NEVERTHELESS, WE PERSISTED

NEVERTHELESS, WE PERSISTED

48 VOICES
OF DEFIANCE,
STRENGTH,
AND COURAGE

ALFRED A. KNOPF
New York

THIS IS A BORZOI BOOK PUBLISHED BY ALFRED A. KNOPF

Text copyright © 2018 by In This Together Media
Jacket art copyright © 2018 by Post Typography

All rights reserved. Published in the United States by Alfred A. Knopf,
an imprint of Random House Children's Books,
a division of Penguin Random House LLC, New York.

Knopf, Borzoi Books, and the colophon
are registered trademarks of Penguin Random House LLC.

For additional copyright information, please see page 303.

Some of the names of persons appearing in this book have been changed.

Visit us on the Web! GetUnderlined.com

Educators and librarians, for a variety of teaching tools, visit us at RHTeachersLibrarians.com

Library of Congress Cataloging-in-Publication Data
Title: Nevertheless, we persisted : 48 voices of defiance, strength, and courage.
Description: First edition. | New York : Alfred A. Knopf, [2018]
Identifiers: LCCN 2017043558 (print) | LCCN 2017056383 (ebook) |
ISBN 978-1-5247-7196-6 (trade) | ISBN 978-1-5247-7197-3 (lib. bdg.) |
ISBN 978-1-5247-7198-0 (ebook)
Subjects: LCSH: Conduct of life—Juvenile literature. | Persistence—Juvenile literature. |
Courage—Juvenile literature.
Classification: LCC BJ1631 (ebook) | LCC BJ1631 .N48 2018 (print) | DDC 170/.44—dc23

The text of this book is set in 11.25-point Dante.

Printed in the United States of America
September 2018
10 9 8 7 6 5 4 3 2 1

First Edition

Random House Children's Books supports the First Amendment and celebrates the right to read.

CONTENTS

NEVERTHELESS, WE PERSISTED

FOREWORD

By US Senator Amy Klobuchar

"She was warned. She was given an explanation. Nevertheless, she persisted."

I was on the Senate floor on February 7, 2017, when these words were spoken about my colleague Senator Elizabeth Warren of Massachusetts. Tensions were running high; tempers, too.

"Nevertheless, she persisted."

These words were meant to mark the end of a heated debate, but instead they marked an important beginning.

By the next morning, #ShePersisted was trending on Twitter. A few weeks later, more than one hundred women in my home state of Minnesota lined up to get a tattoo of the words.

"Nevertheless, she persisted" became a rallying cry for anyone who has ever stood up for what's right. The phrase became a real comfort for anyone who has beaten the odds—which is almost everyone. And it became the inspiration for this book—which is filled with powerful essays by people who have persisted.

In these pages, you'll read about a woman who lost her young

1

brother far too early and a paraplegic athlete who coaches wheelchair basketball in war-torn countries. You'll learn from hard-working underdogs, unlikely leaders, and incredible people who took on whatever life threw at them. They all faced adversity. They all rose above it. And they all inspired others to join them on their journeys of hope.

I don't know many lawmakers or leaders who haven't faced adversity. So often, it's that struggle that leads us to lead.

I have a wonderful dad who was a sports reporter and long-time newspaper columnist. But for decades he also battled alcoholism. His addiction took its toll on his life and our family. After his well-publicized arrest for a DWI, I sat down with my dad to tell him all the ways he was hurting both himself and the people he cared about. But I also told him that I loved him and that I knew he could save himself. He did, and he has lived out the last decades of his life sober, grateful, and—to use his own words—pursued by grace.

Years later I was elected prosecutor for Minnesota's largest county. Every day I met families that were being torn apart by the loss of loved ones to drunk drivers. I led the effort to pass Minnesota's first felony DWI law. And now, as a senator, I am taking on the fight to end the opioid epidemic by increasing access to treatment and doing everything we can to prevent addiction before it starts.

I don't want another teenager to have to take the keys from her dad. Or a little kid to have to worry about when his mom is coming home. So when it comes to legislating on this stuff, I won't take no for an answer.

Now, let me tell you, it's not always easy for women to persist in the United States Senate.

Over the course of our nation's history, we have had nearly two thousand men in the Senate—but only fifty women! And twenty-one of those women are serving today. The women of the Senate are the hardest-working, most effective legislators I know. A recent analysis showed that the Senate's women not only introduce more legislation than the men do, they also work better together to get it passed.

Senator Olympia Snowe of Maine led efforts on the budget and taxes for decades. In 2013, Senator Susan Collins, also from Maine, led a group of fourteen senators—six of them women—in presenting a proposal to end the government shutdown. Senator Patty Murray of Washington led the budget negotiations after that.

Senator Debbie Stabenow of Michigan spearheaded the 2014 farm bill. Together, Senators Lisa Murkowski of Alaska and Maria Cantwell of Washington crafted the 2017 energy bill. Senator Barbara Boxer of California shepherded the transportation bill of 2015 through Congress. Senator Dianne Feinstein of California released the report on torture during the Iraq War. Senators Claire McCaskill of Missouri and Kirsten Gillibrand of New York are leading the fight against sexual assault in the military. And all the women of the Senate came together to support my bill to combat human trafficking.

But sometimes the smallest victories are the most memorable. A few years ago, I sent out a tweet that went viral. It said that for the first time in the history of the Senate, we had a traffic jam in the women's bathroom.

That's when Senator Barbara Mikulski of Maryland—then the "dean" of the Senate women—and I appointed ourselves to the Expand the Women Senators' Bathroom Committee.

Soon after, the architect of the Capitol presented us with a plan to add one stall. Barbara looked at the plan and said, "It's a bathroom for the present. We want a bathroom for the future—one for fifty women senators!"

We both looked at the architect, and I said, "That's right. It's a glass-ceiling bathroom plan."

Of course, no one messes with Barbara Mikulski. We got the extra stalls.

The women of the Senate have all beaten the odds. They're all determined to get things done for the American people. And I'd add that not one of them is afraid to take chances, and—even more importantly—none is afraid to fail.

Failure is a big part of persisting. It just is. Ask, well, pretty much anyone. Before Oprah was Oprah, she was fired from her job coanchoring the six o'clock news in Baltimore. Before Bill Gates launched Microsoft, he had a company called Traf-O-Data. Ever heard of it? Me neither. In fact, Ben & Jerry's has a Flavor Graveyard for all those "dearly de-pinted" flavors that have been pulled from store shelves.

It's important to try. Sometimes it will work out. Sometimes it won't. But then you've got to get back up and try again.

You see, obstacles don't just challenge us. They change us. They shift the way we view the world, help us grow stronger, and even encourage us to make friends we might not otherwise have.

I once heard the story of a humor writer, Jane Lotter of Seattle, who developed terminal cancer and decided to write her own obituary. In it, she left her children with this wisdom: "May you always remember that obstacles in the path are not obstacles, they *are* the path."

No one welcomes more adversity in life. But adversity is a part of life. It is the path. So the only way we can make a difference—in our lives and in the world around us—is to keep working, keep fighting, and keep persisting.

I hope you'll take the stories in this book to heart. Learn from these experiences. Follow these examples. Know that you're not alone.

Because nevertheless, *we* persist.

 US Senator Amy Klobuchar is the first woman elected to represent Minnesota in the United States Senate. She ranked first in the Senate with the most bills enacted into law during the 114th Congress.

SOMEWHERE OVER THE RAINBOW

By Sally Kohn

In 1974, a gay man named Gilbert Baker met the prominent gay rights leader Harvey Milk, who, four years later, would be assassinated just months after becoming one of the first openly gay people ever elected to public office in the United States. Milk challenged the gifted designer to come up with a symbol for gay pride. And so Gilbert Baker created the rainbow pride flag.

The rainbow flag has been the international symbol of gay pride ever since, and when I was in college in the late 1990s, I owned every decorative rainbow flag item imaginable. I went to college at the George Washington University in Washington, DC, only a few hours away from my hometown of Allentown, Pennsylvania, but light-years away culturally. Allentown had one small gay bar with blacked-out windows. Washington had a whole gayborhood, with bars and restaurants and coffee shops. And stores. Where I bought all the rainbow stuff. I had earrings and necklaces and T-shirts and socks and shoelaces and you name it. All of which I often wore at the same time.

I wanted the entire world to know that I was gay—very gay—and proud of it.

My parents were always supportive, from the moment I came out of the closet in high school to every month during college when, thankfully, they paid the bill for the credit card that paid for all the rainbow stuff. They also helped pay for flights to visit my high school girlfriend, who was in college in Massachusetts and whose parents had openly disapproved of us both when they found out about our relationship. So I had this strange mix: my own parents being intensely loving and supportive, my girlfriend and I sneaking around behind her parents' backs. Still, many kids had it way worse, and even my girlfriend's parents eventually begrudgingly accepted us—though years later, when we were living together, they would visit and literally not talk to me, so that was weird. But like I said, others had it worse.

Which is to say, other than my girlfriend's resentful parents, I'd never really dealt with anything I felt to be homophobia. Despite the larger climate of homophobia in America in the 1980s and 1990s, I had a gay-friendly family. I went to a pretty gay-friendly high school where there were other openly gay kids and couples. And then I went to a gay-friendly college in a gay-friendly city where, every Halloween, drag queens raced in high heels down the main street in the gayborhood. I was living a charmed, pride-flag-laden gay life.

Or that's how I remember it, anyway. Reality was a bit more complicated. I felt that my girlfriend's parents really hated me and my existence, and certainly our relationship, and they were a constant source of strain. And all around me there was a growing reactionary right-wing movement and a rising cultural backlash against the sorts of acceptance and progress I felt in other parts of my life. And then there was one afternoon during my freshman year, when I came home from class to find that someone had written a homophobic epithet on the message board on my dorm room door. I actually don't remember what it was. I think it was *faggot,* but I really don't remember. And that's the point. At the time, I was devastated, furious, shattered. I thought I'd come to this gay mecca, far away from my girlfriend's hateful parents and the anguish they caused me, surrounded by cool, cosmopolitan kids who all were down with the gay thing. And then someone pierced my bubble with a single word scrawled on my door. I remember calling my girlfriend and crying, and that there was a dorm meeting to address it. I remember how insecure it made me feel, like the sense of support I felt could disappear at any moment. And all that would leave me with was my still-insecure, searching, grasping little self—not really knowing who I was or how to be proud of myself on my own, decorating with pride to disguise my own internal discomfort. Which at that age wasn't about being gay, or *just* about being gay, but about everything. I remember all those feelings, the fear and sadness. But I can't for the life of me remember what actual word it was that hateful person wrote on my door.

Because it all feels a million miles away now. The epithet. The girlfriend's parents. The rainbow flags. I actually see pride earrings in stores now and have to stifle some sort of gag reflex, not only sartorial but political—because I can't believe I ever wore a necklace made out of metal rainbow links, or felt that I had to. I'm not less gay now, not at all. Maybe even the contrary, now that I'm a public figure and a very publicly gay one at that. But my fledgling sense of my identity—my definition of myself in the face of hostility and thus my desire to clad myself in a sort of armor of pride—feels so sad to me now. Back then, I too often let others define me—including those who didn't approve of my life or my choices. The hate from my girlfriend's parents and that person who wrote on my door encircled me, imprisoned me, had way more power over my consciousness and sense of self than I could admit. I put on the gay pride paraphernalia on the outside because I couldn't always muster what I needed on the inside. Pride was something to buy because it wasn't something I had.

And yet, just twenty years later, I can't precisely remember what that hateful word was that was scrawled on my dorm room door. Half my life later and I'm now called way worse words on a pretty much daily basis, and I couldn't care less. My sense of self is strong and only growing. I have a partner—whom I met after college and whose parents are loving and supportive—and together we have a daughter and a dog and a community of friends, all of whom are as accepting and loving as I ever could have hoped for. And yet even then it doesn't matter as much—because I love and accept myself more than my teenage self ever could have dreamed, not just the gay parts but all the parts, the parts I thought were rough and weird and unfortunate and now appreciate as what makes me uniquely, wonderfully me. I don't remember what that person wrote on my door all those years ago because I don't care anymore. Their hate doesn't define me. I define myself.

After a spate of suicides by teens a few years ago, gay, lesbian, bisexual, and transgender adults started sharing messages that It Gets Better. And I remember thinking: *It* all *gets better.* Not just being gay. Everything. Every second that I'm alive, I become more comfortable in my own skin, more okay with my own faults and foibles, more enthusiastic about my gifts and ambitions. And more genuinely proud, not because I bought pride at a store to put on myself, but from something I found within. Eventually. With time.

I wish I could go back and tell my younger self that it would all be okay, that the problems that seemed so big then would eventually fade to the point of forgetting—that instead of swallowing and internalizing hate and anger, I would grow strong enough to fight them. And yet, in my way, I did persist even then. I stayed with that girlfriend for several years after high school—in spite of, or perhaps because of, her parents' hate. And I wore that damn gay pride paraphernalia like I was a float in my own parade, defying the world around me with every bead and thread. And that resistance was beautiful and brave in its own way—even if it was tacky.

 Sally Kohn is a CNN political commentator and columnist.

FOR BROWN GIRLS WHO BLOSSOM ON THEIR OWN TIME

By Prisca Dorcas Mojica Rodriguez

School was always hard for me. I was never the straight-A student. I wanted to be that student really badly, but no matter how much I tried, school was just too hard.

I remember my first day of second grade like it was yesterday. I walked in very hesitant, because I was scared to go to a new school in this new country. But I was also really excited, because I loved making new friends and I just wanted to find out who these new friends were going to be. I had no idea that I should also be worrying about the fact that I simply had not learned how to read yet and could not keep up with these second graders. I was eight years old and did not even know what letters looked like. The alphabet was a mystery to me.

When—upon the quick discovery that I could not find my seat because I could not even read my own name—I was taken out of my second-grade class and walked into a first-grade class, I saw that school was less about making friends and more about trying to keep up with my peers.

Nobody spoke to me and told me that this was not my fault. I do not remember being told that I had nothing to be ashamed of; everyone just focused on getting me to catch up to the first graders. What this meant was that I felt dumb for a really long time. I think I needed someone in my corner telling me I was doing enough.

By the time I was a junior in high school, I had learned that learning was something you did in only one type of way—otherwise you were discarded as dumb. My parents' lack of formal education meant that I was seeing and hearing concepts for the first time in my classroom, so school was always about catching up with white, upper-middle-class definitions of excellence.

During my junior year, I began to hear about college. Yes, *hear* about college, through the college-bound kids, because college was not something that was encouraged and foretold for everyone in my school. Nobody was going up to me directly and telling me that I should apply to college. I was not being asked where I expected to go to college. In fact, when one of my teachers did ask me about college, I looked away and smiled nervously because I thought: *Why is she asking me that? Didn't anyone tell her that I am not one of those people?* I had begun to accept that I myself was just not one of those kids, through years of never getting the A's and of being an older student in my class.

But because I am a deep processor, I decided to ask around. I began to pay close attention to who those college-bound kids were and what they were doing differently. The thing that stood out the most was that those college-bound kids were entrenched in Advanced Placement classes. When most seniors I knew were working half the day outside school or taking easy classes like (as we joked) underwater basket weaving, the AP students were stressing out over their grades and their schoolwork, even during the peak of senioritis.

So, having learned that the students in the AP classes were the college-bound ones, I knew what I had to do once I had decided that I, too, would be going to college.

I walked up to my assigned school counselor and gave him the list of classes I had chosen for my senior year, a list of only AP classes. I was ready, I had accepted the challenge: I, a mediocre student of color whom nobody expected much out of, was going to go to college. And while I did not know what going to college really meant, I knew that I was going to do it.

My counselor informed me that he did not approve of my class selection. He looked at my 2.5 GPA and looked at my request and did everything but laugh in my face. He said something about how some kids are book smart, and other kids, kids like me, possess a different type of intelligence. What I have is called kinetic intelligence, meaning I'm good at sports.

I sat there bewildered, because I was no star athlete. This man knew nothing about my level of "kinetic intelligence" but had made assumptions based on what he saw, which was a girl whose body was genetically fit but not actually accustomed to running or kicking soccer balls any sort of commendable distance. I sat there confused and hurt, because I knew that somehow he probably felt really good about himself for having insulted me in such a graceful way. I also knew, like any other public school kid, that if you wanted something really badly, and the school refused to listen to you, bringing in your parents was always the solution. So I left his office determined to get my *mami* on board.

I remember the enthusiasm with which I told my *mami*, after I raced home that day, that I was trying to go to college. I remember her confused smile, and her telling me that she supported me. I told her that the counselor was not letting me take the classes I needed to take in order to make my dreams come true, and she said that she would come to the school to speak to him. I was elated!

The next day, when I got called to my counselor's office, I walked down the halls like someone who knew that her *mami* was on her side. I walked proud and I walked ready.

I sat next to my Spanish-speaking *mami,* ready to translate for her. My counselor proceeded to take out my class request form, and he said in a much more polished tone than he had used with me the day before that he advised me not to take all these AP classes. He said that with my GPA, putting me in more difficult classes would set me up for failure. He said that with non-English-speaking parents, I was at a disadvantage, because my peers in those classes would have support at home. My parents' immigration status meant that their efforts were not enough, comparatively.

He paused for me to translate to my *mami* all that he had said. So I turned to my *mami* and translated what this man was *actually* saying about me, and us. I told her: *"Este hombre piensa que soy estúpida, y que no debo tomar clases difíciles porque ustedes no saben inglés y no me pueden hacer mi tarea. Este hombre esta insultándonos."*

And then I paused and waited for her reply—which, I predicted, would be a fiery one. But here's the thing about internalized racism and internalized oppression: it cuts your wings off before you've even been taught that you have any. So my *mami* looked at me with concern and said: *"Tal vez este hombre tiene razón."*

My chest felt like it collapsed. I was immediately sweating, and was on the verge of crying. This stranger knew nothing about me, and I was okay with what he had misread about my potential, but my *mami*'s doubt made me begin to doubt myself.

And in the longest ten seconds of my life, I decided that college was going to be in my future and it did not matter that no one believed in me. I cannot really verbalize why this was the decision I made for myself. I just knew that going to college meant good things for me, and I was going to believe in myself for all the adults who didn't. I turned to my counselor and translated what my *mami* would have said if systematic oppression had not clipped her wings: "My mom said that you will put me in those AP classes, and I will be okay."

On that day I was placed in AP classes, and the following school year I entered those classes scared but ready. Later I ended up applying to, attending, and graduating from a four-year university.

From that experience I learned that for people like me, having dreams is a gift, and pushing against the odds is a social curse that someday will no longer exist, because enough *malcriada* brown girls will have paved the way for new possibilities.

 Prisca Dorcas Mojica Rodriguez is a writer who started the online platform Latina Rebels.

OWN WORLD

By Alia Shawkat

I grew up splitting my time between Palm Springs and Los Angeles. Palm Springs, in the California desert, is where I was born and raised. I lived with my folks and my two brothers, and my grandparents lived next door. And I started acting professionally at a young age, so my mom and I would drive up to Los Angeles for auditions, sometimes as often as four times in one week. I was always adjusting to new environments, constantly going back and forth between feeling like a kid at school and like an adult on set.

My middle school in the desert was a private school with only ten kids in my class. Kyle, a Korean boy, and I were the only nonwhite kids. We were also best friends. I never realized until we got older why we were considered different. We were left out and didn't connect with the other kids. Bullying words and actions were the norm, but Kyle and I had fun in our own worlds and imaginations. We imagined the Spice Girls coming to save us.

This was around the time I started acting, and it wasn't the easiest entrance. My mom would send my head shots to agents in the city, and we wouldn't hear anything back. She finally called to make sure the photos were being received. My father is Iranian, and when my mother finally reached someone, she was told that I looked "too ethnic" for the parts they were trying to cast, and that's why we weren't getting any responses. But we were determined. We drove to Los Angeles and I auditioned for the agents in person. I was able to prove that I was talented enough to get an opportunity, and I started working right away.

Once I started high school, I was going to Los Angeles more frequently for work, and I began to hate my time in the desert. I never wanted to go back to school and do homework when adults were treating me with respect all week. I got to hang with a kid my own age on set and act out fun scenes with a real crew. It was beyond exciting. Then I'd have a break from the biz and get shipped back to the desert. Kids there didn't care where I had been or what I was doing. They surmised that I was full of myself, too cool for school after having been gone for most of the year. At this point, I cared a lot about what other kids thought of me. I was insecure in my curly hair and pudgy face. I wanted to slip into a disguise in which I could look like these skinny, clean-haired girls and walk with abandon. But I knew I was appreciated for my differences somewhere else. The world of Hollywood, which had initially rejected me because I was too different, became my sanctuary.

The two worlds I grew up in altered my perspective of myself. On the one hand, I was told how cute and talented I was. I dressed up, had makeup put on every day, got to make creative choices, and hung out with some of the funniest people I had ever met. I had responsibilities and the freedom to express my-self. On the other hand, I was just a kid who couldn't keep up with her homework, missed social engagements, and couldn't maintain friendships. My mom always made a point to take me back to the desert the minute I finished shooting. At the time, all I wanted to do was stay in Los Angeles and hang with my new actor friends—but looking back, I'm so happy she did that. I realize that the balance I was struggling with was exactly what I needed to find my own truth about how I wanted to be seen and treated. Hollywood and the lifestyle of an actor can be just as tricky as high school. People give you attention one day and forget your name the next.

When I graduated from high school, I moved to New York. The show I was shooting had ended, and now these two worlds I was trying to find myself in were done. I had plans for college, but I withdrew quickly. I finally had my own time to be the art-ist I wanted to be. Then, for the first time since I was a kid, I stopped working. The simplicity with which I had viewed acting had become much more complicated. I felt an aversion to the way girls my age were propped up and advertised. Blond, skinny, with straight hair. It reminded me of the high school girls who never accepted me. I wanted no part of it. I would go on auditions, and I would get feedback that I seemed like I didn't want to be there. That was the truth. I didn't see myself in any of those roles. I was always sent out to be an apathetic, insecure teen, or the insecure fat friend who makes a joke every now and then to her perfect blond friend who goes on to find love. Not only was my ego being bruised, I didn't like those stories. Nothing felt interesting or im-portant to me. I was also taking myself way too seriously. I had started to paint, which helped release my angst, but I was very bitter toward acting, and Hollywood in general. I now saw that it was just another version of high school, and once again, I was not embraced.

A year passed, during which I truly thought I would quit the biz for good to focus on a different form of expression. Or get a job that didn't rely so heavily on self-awareness and ego. I continued painting, and went on tour with my then boyfriend. Then I got an audition for a film called *Whip It*, about a girl from a small town who gets involved in Roller Derby despite the fact that her parents want her to be in beauty pageants instead. The role I was auditioning for was Pash, the ethnic best friend. Sure, I didn't want to be typecast, but this film was all about women who strove for what they wanted. Ellen Page was cast as the lead, and I went in to read with her. I never prepped more for an audition in all my life. I was so ready. I was Pash.

I got the part. I became great friends with Ellen and all the amazing, strong-ass women I met on set. I realized that if I judged the world based solely on the stereotypes it promoted, I would always feel stuck. Since that job, I have worked just as hard as I did on that audition to collaborate with like-minded people and be open to projects that I feel support the same ideas and beliefs that I have.

At twenty-eight, I am now the lead of my own show, one on which my ethnicity and weight are not addressed. I'm the storyteller. Just like each person is in his or her own life. I hope to keep my judgment at bay and continue to pursue art that feels right and honest. As I get older, I'm constantly adjusting how I view myself, the world, and others. Now I am seeing other people and artists make work that I always wanted to see and be a part of. There will always be a confusion in finding a balance between how you express yourself and what is welcomed by others, but that specific path is what makes a place for you. A place all your own.

 Alia Shawkat is an actress known for her roles in the television series Arrested Development *and* Search Party, *the film* Green Room, *and many more productions.*

YOUR GOLDEN THREAD

By Matthew Burgess

Wearing silver moon boots, pajamas, and a towel around my head in a nod to the iconic Go-Go's album cover, I press play on the boom box and strut into the room to Michael Jackson's "Wanna Be Startin' Somethin'." My sister, cocooned in a blanket on the couch, looks over and sizes me up. I flip off the television and moonwalk to center stage: "I said you want to be startin' some-thin' / You got to be startin' somethin'." The dog joins in, barking and nipping, so I grab his front paws and cha-cha until he shakes free and flees. Then the tower of towel tips, and I can see that my makeshift performance is doing the trick: Karen has cracked a smile. I helicopter my sweatshirt over my head and fling it into the kitchen striptease-style, kick one boot off at a time, and finally my sister—still seated but bouncing—joins me in chanting the song's climactic gibberish: "Ma ma se, ma ma sa, ma ma coo sa." Again and again and again—punctuated by Michael's exuberant shrieks—until the song ends and I collapse beside her on the cushions.

We both feel better for the moment, but the dark cloud will descend again soon. And though it didn't occur to me then, Michael Jackson's lyrics can be read as a description of what grief often feels like:

> *It's too high to get over (yeah, yeah)*
> *Too low to get under (yeah, yeah)*
> *You're stuck in the middle (yeah, yeah)*
> *And the pain is thunder (yeah, yeah)*

Six months earlier, a close friend of the family had been killed by a drunk driver in front of her three children. The driver's friend had been sitting in the passenger seat with a video camera, and they had been filming unsuspecting pedestrians as they sped toward them and then away at the last moment. Then they would go home, play the tape, and laugh at people's frightened reactions. This was their twisted game, and when Debbie stepped into the alleyway behind her house where her children had been playing, holding one hand up in a gesture to slow the car down, the driver allegedly lost control of the vehicle and slammed into her. She died in the hospital hours later.

I was fourteen at the time, and my sister Karen was twenty-three. We were both very close to Debbie, and losing her—combined with the tragic and senseless circumstances of her death—hit us hard.

Debbie had been my babysitter when I was a baby, the youngest of five children. She stepped into that chaos and picked me up. She seat-belted me into her Volkswagen and drove me around town like a golden retriever puppy. She took me to the beach and set me down in the sand with a shovel and a pail. She handed me baggies of Cheerios and Pepperidge Farm Goldfish crackers. Years later she got married, had her own kids, and moved to a house by the beach. And then, when I was in the seventh grade, I started babysitting for *her* kids. I remember when Debbie and her husband would come home after a night out, he would disappear upstairs to check on the kids and Debbie would drive me home. She'd ask me questions about my life and we'd have long conversations in the dark car while crossing the bay in the auto ferry. What I remember most about Debbie is that she didn't talk to me from across that divide that often exists between kids and "grown-ups." I didn't have that connection with many others, so it felt like a rare, important thing. There was no authority in her voice, no grown-up apartness. I could speak openly, and she always made me laugh and feel at ease.

The morning after Debbie died—just hours after the initial shock—I got dressed in a never-before-worn uniform for the first day of high school. I didn't feel up for it, but I went, and I did my best to put on the face of a regular freshman. Everything felt hollow, distant, eerie, swimmy—I didn't fully grasp it at the time, but now I recognize these feelings as normal symptoms of shock and grief. I don't remember processing Debbie's death with anyone or talking about it at length; mostly I went through the motions and did what was expected of me. The first few months of high school definitely were a distraction—every day was packed with classes, homework, practice, friends—and I probably had reached a point at which I was more or less "okay" when death struck a second time.

Less than four months after Debbie was killed, Karen's boyfriend was in the back seat of a Volkswagen Beetle when the driver lost control and rolled across the freeway in Los Angeles. Karen was out of state with my mother visiting our cousins at the time, and while they were on the flight home, my father received the phone call. He picked me up from school and told me the news—Michael had been in an accident and was in the intensive care unit. I remember trying to convince myself that he would be fine. "But Michael's okay, right? He's going to be okay? It's a car accident. People are in car accidents all the time and they are fine." The look on my dad's face said otherwise, but I blocked myself from the full weight of the news until we arrived home and he told my sister. The sounds that came from her that night—*keening* was a word I would learn later—I could never unhear.

My family gathered at our house within hours—one sister drove up from San Diego and another drove down from Los Angeles—to form a supportive circle around Karen. In three separate cars, we caravanned to the hospital. The events that followed are blurry, but I remember listening in on a discussion about whether and when to take Michael off life support. Brain function had stopped; he was being kept alive by the machines. This didn't make any sense at all. I could hear Michael's laugh in my head. He was so young, so fun to be around, so twinkly-eyed. Michael was the kind of guy you could lean against while watching a movie on the couch, trade bites of your ice cream with, sing along with to Top 40 songs with the windows down on the way to the beach.

Two of the brightest, funniest, and most radiantly alive human beings in my life had been killed, suddenly and under circumstances that shattered my sense of how the universe was supposed to operate. I had a ton of questions but felt too paralyzed to ask them. "God," as I was led to understand "him," no longer made sense. (Where was the mercy? Where was the protection?) Meanwhile, none of the so-called grown-ups in my life seemed to have much salvaging wisdom to offer. Or if they did, they didn't

28

know how to cross the divide. How to open the door of the closet that I was in, sit beside me on the floor in the dark, and slowly initiate a conversation.

After Michael's funeral, Karen moved back home with my parents and me. As the youngest of five siblings, I was the last one left in the nest, and now Karen was back until further notice. We all did what we could to comfort her. My mother cooked dinners. My father came home earlier. I tried to cheer her up and make her laugh—hence the late-night dance routines. And my oldest sister, an artist who had lost a boyfriend in college in a motorcycle accident, gave Karen a series of gifts. One was a book that I picked up and held in my hands: Rainer Maria Rilke's *Sonnets to Orpheus*.

At this point my exposure to poetry had been limited. Shel Silverstein's books were on the shelf (and don't get me wrong, I was and remain a fan), but little else. I didn't identify as a writer yet, much less a poet, yet something nudged me to open this book and see what was inside. And though I didn't really understand what I was reading, those words, lines, and images started working their magic on me.

Rilke had written the sonnets after his daughter's childhood friend died at age nineteen, and the poems spoke to my current situation. Death was here, but also beauty. A shaft of light stole into the closet. Suddenly I felt less freaked out, less alone, more curious. Many years later, after becoming a poet myself, I read Donald Hall's definition of a poem as "one inside talking to another inside." In retrospect, I believe this is what happened when I picked up *Sonnets to Orpheus*. Even though those poems had been written in 1922 and translated from Rilke's native German into English, the voice in those lines reached across time and space to the fifteen-year-old me in Southern California. Inside was talking to inside in a way that I had never experienced, and the exchange was transformative. My world suddenly expanded beyond what was immediately visible, and some vital and lifesaving process was set in motion. What else was out there to be discovered?

As you might have guessed, the boy in silver moon boots trying to cheer up his beloved, depressed sister was—surprise, surprise—gay. And while it may be accurate to say that I was "in the closet" at the time, the closet that I found myself in wasn't exclusively about my emerging sexual desires or identity. I was also concealing my sadness, my loss of faith, and the growing suspicion that the world might not be a safe or desirable place to inhabit.

If *closet* signifies a metaphorical inner space where we keep our secrets in shadow, an enclosure inside the self where we are hidden yet at the same time more authentically ourselves, then surely many young people can relate to this experience. Too many of us move through the world feeling freaked out and afraid that who we are on the inside is somehow wrong, shameful, or unacceptable. We worry that if other people really knew us, if they were able to see through our closet into our inside life, then we might be cast out of the nest. In some cases our fears may be exaggerated, but sometimes they are based on reasonable evidence. The people around us, family members included, may not be the most tolerant, enlightened, or open-minded individuals. We might be afraid to be more fully ourselves precisely because we've learned from experience that our immediate environment isn't always safe, accepting, or nurturing of who we are.

Nevertheless, we persist. And one of the things that sustains us is the hunch, the intuition, and eventually the knowledge that we are not alone at all. This realization begins when insides begin talking to insides—whether the communication takes the form of a poem, a song, a conversation, or an essay.

If you are courageous and patient, you will find your tribe. If you give yourself permission to love what you love—whether it is literature, musical theater, drag, or roller disco—kindred spirits will appear. Some will be found in books or in the works they left behind, while others will turn up in the form of living, flesh-and-blood friends. Bullies, zealots, and corporations will try to convince you that if you don't fit in and get with the (*their*) program, you'll be sad and alone. But they have it backward. Your intense and intricate particularity is what the world needs, not your conformity to ways of being or living that feel at odds with your heart. Whatever you think is most unacceptable or unworthy about yourself is usually the source of your magic. The one-of-a-kind youness that makes you you—this is your golden thread.

Yes, the universe can seem frightening, unstable, even cruel, but it can also be beautiful, mysterious, and inspiring. One of the abilities that we as human beings possess is that we can make something out of our experience. We are not merely the effect of our environment; we can be creators. We can respond to what happens and make something that might reach, touch, communicate with another person. We get to participate in this ongoing conversation with kindred spirits across time and space, and the more we do, the more we seek out and attract the kinds of connections that make us feel less anxious and more at home. Instead of living under someone else's rules, we can cocreate the kinds of spaces we wish to inhabit—where insides talk to insides, and we feel grateful to be in such extraordinary company.

 Matthew Burgess is a poet, a picture-book author, and an assistant professor at Brooklyn College.

AS IS

By Alysia Reiner

I never know how to begin something like this, how to start
    I hate beginnings
    They scare the shite out of me
    Here is why
    There is a voice in my head that says
    You are not cool enough
    You are not smart enough
    You are not a good enough writer
    You are dyslexia
    You can't spell
    You are not famous enough
    Nobody cares about what you have to say (actually gives a
shite)
    You are worthless
    You are stupid
    You are too fat, ugly, dumb, old, untalented
    And then I persist.

The biggest lesson in life I have ever learned, the deepest lesson I want to teach my daughter, is to persist. To not listen to those voices, to talk back and tell them to shut up. To move forward, to get back up. So I am writing this for her.

Last night I was at a party. People wanted to take their picture with me. People wanted to take pictures of me. People recognized me. People told me they love me, they love my show, they love my work, they love my acting, they love the film I produced, they love what I do for women. That happens every day. And the same day, an old friend—someone I went to high school with—saw me and told me how beautiful I look. And I swear on my daughter's life I thought to myself: *Fucking liar—fucking Hollywood liar.*

I *could* feel sad about that. Poor me. Poor baby. I was so bullied. I was treated like shite for so long, I just can't believe the good stuff.

Or I could use it as fodder. Kindling for the fire in my belly. To fight for the underdog. To fight for justice and equity for all. *To be love. To be compassion.*

I am writing this essay for the little girl who still believes she sucks. For all girls who question their worth. For all people who question their worth.

And for my daughter.

I was so young when I started getting teased. We call it bullying now, but back then it was just teasing. I remember rumors that I weighed two hundred pounds before I was even nine. I remember never wearing the right thing, never being in the right crowd, always being picked last for every team. Never being invited to anything. Back then there were no rules about inviting all the kids in your class. You could leave out the two losers. And I was always one of them. I was too fat, too tall, too shy. I was so uncomfortable in my own skin, it hurt.

At home my parents fought constantly and worked all the time. I was a latchkey kid, so it felt like my dad was the TV and my mom was a huge plate of Hostess Ho Ho cakes, and I could swear the filling inside a Twinkie tasted like a kiss. I still thank god for the TV shows of my youth and those sweet treats. They kept me from drugs, alcohol, even suicide—which some of my friends chose instead.

I was about eight when I went on my first diet. I mean one I put myself on, instead of the ones everyone always had me on. I can't actually remember a time in my childhood when I wasn't on a diet of one kind or another. I was never allowed bread or pasta or sweets. The famous story of my childhood was when my mom left me with my grandparents for some months as an infant, and when she got back, the first thing she said was, "She's so fat!"

I want to defend that child. That *baby*. That innocent child who wasn't accepted, who learned way too early she wasn't okay *as is*. I want to hold that baby in my arms and hug her and love her and tell her I love her no matter what and she is so beautiful no matter what. I am still healing that baby girl.

After years of trying (*and failing at*) all the diets everyone else put me on, in my teens I got creative and made up my own. The one-apple-a-day diet. The Diet-Coke-and-Trident diet. The soup diet. The chew-and-spit-out diet. The one-bite-of-everything-and-then-put-dish-soap-on-it diet. I was maybe most proud of inventing the condiments diet: you could have unlimited condiments—just nothing to put them on.

I do remember feeling like I wasn't supposed to be doing this. I remember feeling like it was all supposed to be a secret, and I have no idea why. Did I want people to think I just magically lost all this weight? I started trying diet pills I ordered from the back of *Cosmo*, laxatives, exercising in the middle of the night.

My life got soooo small. It was all about the rules of the latest diet. And numbers. Number of calories. Number of days without sugar. Sizes. If only I was thinner, I would be invited. I would have a boyfriend. I would get good grades. If only I got thin . . . my life would be *perfect*.

The voice is up again. This is so boring, everyone knows this story, everyone has this story, everyone felt like this, this is so stupid. I am so boring. I am such a bad writer. Who do I think I am?

I was tall from a very early age, never gangly because I was never thin, and around nine or ten, I grew my nose. Just like my first diet, I can't remember exactly when it changed, what the moment was when I suddenly had a nose that was not the cute-as-a-button variety babies are born with. I don't remember noticing it myself. I was just trying to navigate being a kid, going from pretending and Barbies to homework and mean girls, but suddenly strangers were telling me about my nose. Distant aunts and uncles started asking if I was going to have it fixed, or actually, *When are you going to have it fixed?* So many people not asking me how I felt about my face, but telling me, *There is something wrong with your face.* I had doctors offer to do it for free. That still blows my mind. I felt like the elephant girl. I wanted to hide for the rest of my life.

And yet I wasn't sure I wanted it fixed. I was willing to starve myself to change my body, do anything to try to make myself thin, but I felt strongly that if the universe gave me this nose, this was the nose I was meant to go through life with. And I was starting to get attention from men, grown men. If they thought I was pretty, then maybe I was—even if the boys my age acted as if I was invisible.

I was in high school now and all the girls around me had boobs—excuse me, forgot I'm a grown-up for a second there—

breasts. I was flat as a pancake—maybe throw a couple of chocolate chips on there, but no melons, apples, or grapefruits. I did all those silly chest exercises to try to make them grow. I would pray to god or whomever to make them grow.

So here I was, the chubby girl with a big nose, no boobs, and a huge supply of diet pills, laxatives, and self-hate. And the only kid in my class with parents who were divorcing, as if I needed another reason to hate myself.

It's hard for me to recall all this—to write it down—in part because I have worked quite hard to let it go. One of my favorite acting teachers of all time, Ian Tucker, once told a class I was in that as actors, we have to be brilliant shedders. We have to shed the last audition, the fight with our lover, the subway being late, the insult about our nose, the cruel comments about our lack of thigh gap. Otherwise we walk into the room to audition with huge, heavy bags—like dragging in five-hundred-pound duffel bags full of self-hate, self-doubt, and crappy history and asking the casting director or producer or director to hold our bags while we audition. *No one wants to hold our baggage.* It's really freaking heavy. So I learned to let go.

How?

How did I learn to let go and get back up?

How did I learn to believe in myself?

I won't bore you with all the details, but the eating disorder got really bad. I was probably clinically depressed, and my dad's second wife caught me stealing laxatives out of their bathroom and told me about OA, the twelve-step program that teaches you how to get out of an addiction to overeating.

I have never talked in the media about being in a program. I am pretending as I write this that it will stay private. You guys won't tell, right? But I think it's important.

How did I get to this moment, free of plastic surgery, with only a small sachet of self-doubt?

I found acting. I found a place where I could get out of my own body and be anyone or anything. I found an incredible acting teacher in high school, Peter Royal, who taught me how to serve art and led me on the lifelong journey of getting out of my own way.

I found literature and lots of characters in books who felt like I did. I think it started with *The Story of Ferdinand* and led to Judy Blume. Karen in *It's Not the End of the World* was my BFF. *Blubber* was my homegirl. Suddenly I didn't feel so alone.

I kept finding amazing books that gave me a little hope. I never really was into video games but I had friends who were, and sometimes I felt like I was living a game of old-school *Super Mario Bros.* and I kept finding gold coins on the road that sustained me. The self-help section of the local bookstore saved my life. My tools were *The Artist's Way, Jonathan Livingston Seagull,* Wayne Dyer, Oprah, Deepak Chopra. When I met my husband, David, just out of my teens, he was reading *The Road Less Traveled.* I thought he was just pretending to read it to pick up chicks, but he was actually reading it, and we bonded over the desire to grow ourselves.

It's funny to us that *woke* is an expression now, because back when I met him doing Shakespeare in Vermont—my first professional job—we started talking about people who want to sleep through life and people who want to be awake. And the thing that I think has kept us together all these years is that we want to stay awake. We promised to wake each other up if either of us fell asleep at the wheel of life.

And I found my people. I found David, but even before him

I went to camp or after-school programs or, of course, the theater at school, and I found the losers and outliers like me, people who cared what I thought, or loved that I was a great listener, or I could make laugh, or would act with me, play with me. My games of pretend from childhood saved me in the end.

So what have I learned? What do I want to tell you? What are the secrets of the universe I wish someone had told me? You get to a certain age and you feel like you have heard it all and you have no wisdom to share, but the clichés are all true.

Yes, you are the only entry in the [insert your name] section of the dictionary.

Yes, persist. Yes, it will get better. Yes, get back up, yes, shed your baggage, yes, think of your life as a video game and look for the treasures, yes, find your tool kit, yes, love yourself as is.

 Alysia Reiner is an actress, a producer, and an activist known for her roles on Orange Is the New Black *and in* Equity.

EVERYONE PLAYS

WORDS: AMY CHU
ART: LOUIE CHIN

I WENT TO HIGH SCHOOL IN THE MIDWEST. IOWA TO BE EXACT.

THIS IS ME. I WAS EXTREMELY SHY BACK THEN.

MOST OF THE KIDS GREW UP THERE AND ALREADY KNEW EACH OTHER.

EVERY SO OFTEN SOMETHING WOULD HAPPEN TO REMIND ME THAT I DIDN'T FIT IN.

GOOK.

I'M CHINESE, NOT VIETNAMESE. IT DIDN'T MATTER THAT HE GOT HIS SLUR WRONG. IT STILL STUNG.

TO MAKE THINGS WORSE, IT WAS PROM TIME. I DIDN'T HAVE A DATE, BUT I STILL WENT.

THE AFTER PARTY WAS AT A POPULAR GIRL'S HOUSE. HER MOTHER WAS ON THE SCHOOL BOARD.

NATURALLY I DROPPED A COCKTAIL SAUSAGE ONTO MY WHITE DRESS. IT ROLLED ALL THE WAY DOWN THE FRONT.

OH NO.

SORRY ABOUT THE MESS.

I THINK IT'LL COME OUT WITH SOME DRY-CLEANING.

I DO WISH YOU WOULD HAVE TALKED WITH THE BOARD FIRST BEFORE YOU SUED US.

SO MUCH FOR FITTING IN.

THINGS GOT EVEN WORSE. ONE COACH REFUSED TO LET HIS TEAM PLAY IF I WALKED ONTO THE FIELD.

HE MADE SURE THE PRESS WAS THERE TO MAKE HIS POINT. MY HUMILIATION WAS COMPLETE.

GIRLS TEAM TRYOUTS!

BUT IN THE END, I WON. THE SCHOOL DECIDED TO SET UP A NEW GIRLS' TEAM.

DOZENS OF GIRLS SHOWED UP FOR THE TRYOUTS.

YEARS LATER, I MOVED TO NEW YORK AND BECAME A WRITER. I PUT THOSE HIGH SCHOOL YEARS BEHIND ME.

ONE DAY I WAS SURPRISED TO GET AN EMAIL ASKING IF I WOULD ATTEND THE DEDICATION OF THE SCHOOL'S NEW SOCCER FIELD.

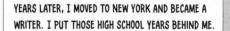

I WAS CURIOUS TO SEE WHAT HAD CHANGED, IF ANYTHING.

THE SAME PRINCIPAL WAS STILL THERE. AFTER ALL THOSE YEARS, HE HAD MELLOWED. WE TALKED LIKE OLD FRIENDS.

MY OLD COACH WAS THERE, TOO.

AND THEN I FINALLY GOT TO MEET THE GIRLS. THEY WERE EXCITED. I WAS EXCITED.

I WAS SURPRISED TO SEE HOW LARGE THE TEAM WAS. IT TURNS OUT NOW EVERYONE *DOES* PLAY. AND THAT JUST MADE EVERYTHING WORTH IT.

Amy Chu is a graphic novelist currently writing the KISS and Red Sonja series, having wrapped up Poison Ivy's first-ever miniseries for DC Comics.

FROM HIGH-JUMPING TO LIFE SUPPORT TO WHEELCHAIR BASKETBALL IN AFGHANISTAN

By Jess Markt

On a sunny August day in 1996, when I was nineteen years old, my whole life changed in an instant. The last thing I remember is a discussion from the night before, making plans to meet friends at a local gym the next day. I was just a couple of weeks from returning for my sophomore year at the University of Oregon, where I was a high jumper on the track-and-field team, a position I'd earned through a walk-on tryout the previous fall and an accomplishment for which I felt a great deal of pride. I'd been training all summer in preparation for what I hoped would be a dramatic improvement in my sophomore year, and daily workouts like the one I was heading to had become a part of my regular summer routine.

I don't remember leaving my parents' house after lunch that afternoon, but I imagine I was smiling—probably chuckling at the fact that, as usual, I was running a few minutes late and would undoubtedly get a thorough ribbing from my friends as a result. I don't remember speeding in my Honda Accord down the narrow, winding road through the woods about a mile away—a route I'd taken hundreds of times before—as I tried to make up some of the time. I don't remember what caused me to lose control of the car and swerve off the right edge of the road. I don't remember careening off a steep embankment and flying into a pine tree, or the deafening crunch of metal as the roof wrapped around the trunk before the car fell more than ten feet to the forest floor. I don't remember trying unsuccessfully to drag myself out of the mangled vehicle—unaware that my seat belt was still buckled—while blood poured out of wounds on my arms and hands from cuts caused by broken glass. I don't remember waving weakly through the broken driver's-side window from inside the car, trying in vain to get the attention of the few passing cars that drove along the rural road over the course of the next hour, hidden from their view by the steepness of the wooded cliff. I don't remember finally being discovered, or paramedics using the Jaws of Life to cut the car open, pulling me out, strapping me down to a gurney, and loading me onto an emergency medical helicopter, or the feeling of levitating above the treetops and racing through the blue sky.

The first thing I do remember is opening my eyes while being wheeled down a gleaming white hallway on a hospital bed. I didn't understand what was happening or how I came to be in such a place, but I immediately noticed that I was unable to move or feel my legs. I asked the nurse who was guiding the bed—coincidentally, the mother of one of my little brother's best friends, whom I'd met a couple of times before—what was going on and why my legs wouldn't work. It was all very strange and surreal. She told me that I had been in a very serious car accident about two weeks before, that I had broken my back and severed my spinal cord, and that I was now paralyzed from the bottom of my chest down.

What?!

I asked her how long it would be before my legs resumed working. She very patiently and straightforwardly explained that my condition was permanent; because of the severity of my injury, I would never walk again and would need to use a wheelchair to get around for the rest of my life.

My mind reeled. Was this a dream? Oddly, it felt too strange to be a dream.

When we reached my hospital room, the nurse left me alone, and I spent the next hour or so digesting the weight of the information I'd just been given. Two weeks had passed—an eternity for everyone by my side as I fought for life against blood infections, a punctured lung, and a bruise on my brain, all in addition to the broken back—but in my mind, I'd gone to bed the night before ready to get up and head to the gym, only to open my eyes to a completely new world.

I didn't question the truth of what the nurse had told me. I accepted right away that my permanent paralysis was a fact—the lack of feeling and function in my legs, no matter how hard I focused on moving them, confirmed she was not exaggerating the gravity of the situation. This was real. What I was confronted with in that pivotal moment of understanding was how I would approach my new physical reality, both mentally and emotionally.

Would I feel angry and bitter that this had happened to me and not someone else? I was a solid student and a generally positive person. I considered myself a loyal friend and someone who tried to do right by other people as often as possible. I was tempted to ask, *Why me? Why not someone else—someone who deserved it more?*

But no. It was better that this had happened to me than to someone else—especially someone I cared about. I knew I was strong enough to handle the injury, and I knew I'd rather bear that burden than see someone I cared about have to do the same. I would not be angry at the world because of the hand I'd been dealt; I'd just have to figure out how to play it the best I could.

Would I be devastated by the loss of my mobility and, with it, all my athletic ambitions? At that moment, I had no idea what being paralyzed would mean, but I knew my high-jumping career was over before it truly got started. I'd redshirted my freshman year—practicing with the team but not participating in official competitions—in order to get stronger, improve my technique, and save a year of athletic eligibility. Now, as a result, I knew I'd never get to jump in an NCAA meet with the green and gold of the Oregon Ducks on my back. It was a momentarily devastating realization. Surprisingly, though, my mind immediately recognized that those physical accomplishments and goals were only part of who I was. I understood that I was still me—and very lucky to be that, given the magnitude of the accident I'd been in. Now I had the opportunity to explore the deeper aspects of myself, the ones that formed the core of who I was. Wasn't this just a challenge, no different from learning to speak Japanese, attempting to master a Rush song on the guitar, or any other pursuit I'd set my mind to, including the athletic ones? I decided that I would not wallow in self-pity for what might have been; I would focus on the possibilities that still were.

Would I feel hopeless about ever regaining the rest of the life I'd known before? I didn't even know when I'd be able to get out of bed, much less whether I'd eventually have the option to return to school. Would my friends still want to be associated with me? Having known most of my college fraternity brothers only a year, I wondered if our bond was strong enough to survive my physical transformation. Even as I wondered this, I realized the question itself was flawed. My friendships had little to do with the superficial aspects that had changed about me; now they, like my relationship with myself, could grow deeper than before. My outlook, buoyed by the certainty that my friends—as well as my family—would be there for me during and after my recovery, allowed me to focus on overcoming the mental and physical barriers to getting back to college. I would not let self-doubt be a barrier to living and embracing life.

I was fortunate that my subconscious offered me this series of choices in such a transformative moment. I can't entirely explain why everything unfolded so clearly in that first hour of conscious awareness of my new life. It was probably a combination of an upbringing by devoted parents who taught me the value of persistence in the face of challenges, an incredible network of support, and the genetics of how my brain was wired. But part of it was a very conscious decision to take unimaginably difficult news and turn it into something positive—an opportunity to see the world and myself in a different way.

In the days that came, I held on to those first philosophical decisions but realized I needed to figure out how to put them to work in the very real-world challenge of getting out of my hospital bed and on with life. I decided to focus on one goal at a time. First, recover enough physically to get out of the hospital. Second, acclimate to life at home and develop some degree of independence. Third, go back to school and finish my degree. Beyond that, I had no idea what would happen, but I decided to keep my focus on the near future and let the rest unfold as it would.

I trusted that if I worked hard, maintained my self-respect, and opened myself to life's possibilities, things would work themselves out for the best.

With the invaluable support of my family, friends, and community, I managed to accomplish each of my early goals and got my life back on track relatively quickly. I attacked physical rehab with the goal of getting out of the hospital (and away from daily breakfasts of gelatinous scrambled eggs) as soon as possible. With the help of my mother, who was thrown into the role of surrogate nurse in the weeks immediately after my return home, I developed a level of physical independence that would allow me to live on my own. I reacclimated to college life after my father—a home remodeler—worked together with my fraternity and a host of his colleagues in the Portland-area construction industry to raise funds and renovate the fraternity chapter house where I'd lived the year prior to make it wheelchair accessible. I moved back to school just six months after the accident, dove into my interest in writing, and parlayed it into a bachelor's degree in English literature. I reintegrated into my social life almost as though nothing had changed, my friends welcoming me back with open arms.

Soon after I graduated, I moved from Eugene back to Portland and landed a job with a high-tech public relations firm, kicking off an exciting career in communications. Everything was coming together. For all this positive movement in my life, though, there was a final element to my recovery—one I didn't realize was missing—that would bring it full circle.

Around the same time that I started my first PR job, the local National Wheelchair Basketball Association team, the Portland Wheel Blazers, invited me to join one of their practices. They'd gotten my name from a friend with whom I'd gone through the physical rehabilitation portion of my hospitalization—who may have mentioned that I was a six-foot-six former college athlete—and were interested in seeing me play. I'd heard people talk about wheelchair basketball during rehab and had regularly shot baskets with friends after returning to college, but I hadn't really considered the possibility of playing the game competitively.

Basketball was the first sport I'd ever loved, so I was intrigued. But I was skeptical as well; would I connect to the game without the running, the jumping, the dunking, and all the other athletic elements I'd loved so much? I decided it was something I needed to at least try.

It took exactly one practice for me to get hooked. Competitive sports and the camaraderie of being part of a team were clearly parts of my life I'd been sorely missing, even though I hadn't allowed myself to realize it until that moment. All those athletic ambitions I'd had before my injury weren't dead after all. It dawned on me after that first practice that wheelchair basketball would be the final piece in my realization of my full postaccident self.

During the ensuing decade, I pursued my passion for wheelchair basketball as a player while continuing to build my career in communications. In 2009, I was approached with a request to travel to Afghanistan to coach a group of aspiring players who had just been introduced to the game and were looking for someone to teach them how to play. It was a once-in-a-lifetime opportunity to take the game that had given me so much and pass that gift along to others, so I swallowed my nervousness about traveling alone to a war zone halfway across the world and said yes. It turned out to be one of the best decisions I've ever made.

I've been going to Afghanistan twice each year ever since and have seen wheelchair basketball blossom there. The league that has grown from the seed of that first small group of players now includes both men's and women's teams across the country and over four hundred players in total. I coach the Afghanistan men's and women's national teams, which proudly represent their country in competition against great teams from around the world. Along the way, my career shifted from communications to working with the International Committee of the Red Cross to build disability sports programs in countries that, like Afghanistan, are dealing with the effects of war. I get to help people with physical disabilities all over the globe discover their own inner strength through sports, the same way I discovered mine, and watch their personal transformations as a result. It's a job that is more beautiful and rewarding than any I could have conceived of or asked for.

If you'd asked the nineteen-year-old me the day before my car accident in 1996 how I would respond if I woke up the next day and found out I would never walk again, I honestly think I would have said I wouldn't have wanted to go on living. I never could have imagined until actually going through the experience how much my life would blossom *because* of that change and the path on which it set me. I look back at the accident now and know, without reservation, that I wouldn't change it for the world.

 Jess Markt coaches the Denver Rolling Nuggets of the National Wheelchair Basketball Association and starts sports programs for physically disabled people in war and conflict zones around the world.

NEVERTHELESS, LOVE PERSISTS

By Danielle Vabner

Dear Noah,

I still vividly remember the day you were born. It was a crisp fall day, just three days before Thanksgiving. I remember cradling you in my arms, just twelve years old myself. I studied your tiny little features, comparing them to your twin sister's. As I examined your delicate little nose, your long, dark eyelashes, your full lips, I wondered who both of you might become. I wondered who *I* might become. I contemplated the lives that lay ahead of us. I contemplated how no matter what you endured in life, you would always have your twin sister by your side. I remember appreciating what a blessing that was.

We all witnessed you grow, little by little. Slowly but surely, you grew into a fearless, self-assured little boy, always the first to take chances. You jumped as high as you possibly could on the trampoline in the backyard, laughing with delight as you were suspended in the air for a split second. Each time we went to the beach, you ran right into the waves, loving every moment. You also had a mischievous side and took great delight in playing pranks on your siblings. I still recall your playful laugh as you tricked one of your sisters, a sound that I sorely miss.

You were also an old soul, always so wise for your age. You asked questions about the meaning of life, about human existence, about God and the universe. While at times you were very much a little boy who talked about his love of tacos and his desire to work at a taco factory, played superhero video games, and watched *Star Wars,* there was a side of you that was mature almost beyond belief. You often surprised us with your use of big words, your thirst for knowledge, and your desire to know more about the world.

All that—your curiosity, your hopes and dreams for the future, and your zest for life—was unfathomably, incomprehensibly cut short on the morning of December 14, 2012. Like the day you were born, the day you were murdered was crisp and chilly, also just days from a major holiday. Roughly seventy miles away, I slept peacefully in my college dorm room, only days from finishing the first semester of my freshman year. It was not until I awoke to several missed calls that I began to develop a sickening feeling in the pit of my stomach. Almost instantly, with just the sight of five missed calls, I knew something was not right. I dialed our mom's number, and as I met the desperation and despair on the other end of the line, I was violently jerked out of my groggy state.

At that moment, we didn't know much. All we knew was that there had been a shooting at the school shortly after you were dropped off. *A shooting?* I remember thinking. *At Sandy Hook Elementary? There's no way.*

In a fog of shock and helplessness, tears streaming down my

face, I threw on a pair of slippers and ran across campus to a friend's dorm room, still in my pajamas. It was almost as if my feet were moving a million miles per hour while my mind was at a complete standstill, failing to process everything I had just learned.

As soon as I reached my friend's dorm room, I was desperate to find out any information I could. I needed to know that all three of you—you and our two sisters—were okay. I couldn't bear the alternative. As we searched for news updates, early reports claimed that a teacher had been shot in the foot. *If this is the worst of it, this means that everyone is okay.* I breathed a sigh of relief.

As the day progressed, however, it began to look less and less hopeful. As I waited breathlessly for updates in a dorm room seventy miles away, it was chaos in Newtown. Countless families, including our own, raced to the firehouse next to the elementary school to reunite with their children. Mom told me that while they had spotted both of our sisters quickly and easily, you were nowhere to be found. Nor were any of your classmates.

I cannot adequately put into words the feelings of shock, grief, disbelief, and denial that followed. In the hours after, CNN reported that some students had fled into the woods next to the school. I prayed that this was the reason your class hadn't been found. However, as the death toll continued to rise, I tried to prepare myself to receive the worst news a sister could ever possibly receive. But the truth is, there *is* no preparing for something like this.

During the next agonizing couple of hours, my friend's mom raced to New Paltz to pick me up and take me back to Newtown. It was during that car ride that I learned that you, a little boy so full of life, love, and curiosity, were no more. And *that* feeling, of finally learning that what I had hoped and prayed would not be true was real, is something I cannot possibly explain. I remember I immediately went into denial, screaming "No, no, that can't be right!" over and over—as if the more I said no, the more I could wish you back to life. Those first days, weeks, and months without you were a complete and utter blur.

Noah, I am, and always will be, so sorry that your life was violently cut short after just six years. I am so sorry that you were murdered while in the right place at the right time, along with your nineteen classmates and six educators. I am also so sorry that one of us couldn't be there to protect you. In the months after the tragedy, I had dreams about saving you. I had dreams that I was able to convince the shooter not to do what he was about to do. I had dreams that you went on to live the life that twelve-year-old me had hoped you would grow up to have.

In the years following December 14, 2012, the memory of my fearless little brother has inspired me to find inner strength I didn't even know I had. A mere month after your murder, I returned to school for the second semester of my freshman year—but something didn't feel right. I couldn't possibly continue to go to school in the very place where I had learned of the tragedy that claimed your life. I took it upon myself to begin researching schools and stumbled upon one: the University of Texas at Austin. I had your bravery, courage, and fearlessness in mind as I filled out a transfer application—and again, months later, as I packed my bags and relocated to a city where I knew nothing and no one.

I had your spirit with me as I delivered various speeches, fighting for common-sense gun laws and speaking at rallies on the University of Texas at Austin campus. I've shared your story—and mine—with hundreds, possibly even thousands. It is because of you that I was inspired to take chances I never would've taken otherwise. You've given me the courage to speak, even when I didn't think I could. You've given me the courage to fight for what's right, to do whatever I can to prevent someone else from losing a smart, mischievous, fearless little brother—or a sister, or a son, or a daughter, or a father, or a mother, or a friend.

It's because of your courage, bravery, and love of life that I am able to persist.

Love,
Danielle

 Danielle Vabner lost her six-year-old brother, Noah, in the Sandy Hook school shooting on December 14, 2012, and is a passionate advocate for gun violence prevention.

(YOUNG) MAN IN THE MIRROR

By Nate Smith

For most of my teenage years, I despised my reflection. I avoided mirrors. I never took pictures. I believed I was ugly: I was short and dark-skinned and skinny, my nose was too big, so were my lips, my face was riddled with zits. My teeth were crooked and gapped, and the braces I wore to help correct them made me look even more hideous.

During this painfully awkward time in my life, I discovered and lost myself in music. I'd play the drums and listen to records for hours and hours. Music was my escape from the reality of my ugliness. In my mind, I was going to be a great drummer, and it didn't matter that I wasn't so handsome, *because I was going to be cool.*

But in the summer of 1990, my journey toward self-acceptance started the way I imagine it does for a lot of teenage boys: I met a girl.

I noticed her the first day of band camp, the summer before my junior year. She was tall—taller than all the other girls in the band. She had a big, bright smile that lit up a room and long jet-black hair that stood out starkly against her cedar-colored skin. Her name was J, and she was new to our school. Our conversations began simply enough; we had similar taste in music and movies. We had a very similar quirky sense of humor. She liked that I could do voices and imitations. I made her laugh and feel welcome in a new place. As soon as she arrived, all the boys in band class set their sights on her, but of all her potential suitors, she took a liking to me. She was the first girl to tell me she thought I was *handsome*—which was hugely important for a kid as awkward as me.

J lived just a few blocks away from me, so we would hang out all the time after band practice. There was a very real physical attraction between us, and it created a tension that came to a head at her house late one summer day when the air was thick with the humidity of an impending thunderstorm. After a long conversation punctuated with awkward pauses and affectionate gazes, I looked at the clouds and knew my folks would be worried about me. I had to be getting home. We slowly walked to the door, where we paused to share the first of what would be many more-than-friendly embraces. With my heart in my throat, I took a leap of faith and leaned in to kiss her. *She let me. She even kissed me back.*

As I left her house, the clouds burst open, and the thunderstorm began. I walked home in the rain, and my feet never touched the ground.

Over the next few weeks, J and I became two peas in a pod. We walked to and from school together, and we talked on the phone for hours. My parents started to notice a change in me, too; I started to take more time getting myself ready for school in the morning. I started to be more finicky when it came time to pick my clothes and shoes. For the first time, I had someone to look good for.

One evening, after a spell of sitting on her couch and reveling in one another's charms, I noticed the sun starting to hang low in the sky. I knew, once again, I had to be getting home soon.

In parting, we shared a long kiss. After, she whispered into my ear, "I love you."

My eyes became wide as saucers, revealing my surprise. *How could she love me?* I thought. *How could a girl this beautiful love me? I'm ugly. I'm small. I'm dark.* I felt unworthy of her love. Reflexively, and sincerely, I opened my mouth and "I love you, too" creaked out.

It was official: I was in love for the very first time.

A few months later, buzz about the junior prom started to make its way through the halls and classrooms. I, of course, began to bring up the subject to J. "It looks like it could be really fun," I'd say to her, ever so casually. I thought it strange that she would always change the subject—and the more I brought it up, the more tense our exchanges became.

One day, walking home from school after band practice, I reached for J's hand. She snatched it away quickly. "What are you doing?" she scolded, looking over her shoulder. "You know I can't hold your hand!" I was absolutely bewildered. We spent all our time together, morning and evening, and now I felt this gulf opening up between us. She was pushing me away.

After walking her home, I finally spoke up. "J, I don't like this. I don't understand why things are one way when we're alone and completely different when we're around other people. . . ."

She stopped and turned the key in her front door. Very matter-of-factly, she said to me:

"Nate, I really do love you. But I can't be seen in public with you. I need a tall guy, someone I look good with in pictures, and someone who's popular. I can't be seen as your girlfriend. You're too short. You're too small. We can still be friends . . . but I can't be your date to the junior prom." With that, she turned and walked through her front door and shut it behind her.

My heart sank to my soles. I was absolutely devastated. I walked home hunched, the wind knocked out of my lungs.

A few days went by and turned into weeks. I would see J at school, and we'd speak to each other cordially, but there was no denying that the ground was shifting beneath me. The gulf between us was widening rapidly as she floated to her new island of cooler, more popular friends. She started to date a guy named Jimmy, who was a star basketball player. He was everything she wanted: tall, handsome, stylish, and athletic. The hallways would light up as they strolled from class to class, hand in hand.

One Friday evening, Mom and Dad were heading out to a dinner party. They loved to get dressed up and have date nights; they'd start getting ready in the early evening—and usually just as the sky was turning black, they'd be heading out. Still reeling from the rejection, I found a quiet spot in my father's study and sat back in his easy chair. He hurriedly breezed past the room, but the weight of it all must have been too easy to read, because he did a double take. His brow furled up and he asked me, "What's the matter, son?"

I told him about all of it—J, junior prom, the feeling of rejection—and he listened. He sat down on his favorite bar stool and reared back. "You know, son, you're not the Lone Ranger. You're not the first person to be rejected. I thought I was in love once, and I was turned away, too. . . ."

He went on to tell me about his high school sweetheart, how deeply in love he was with her, how she made it clear to him that there was no future for the two of them—and how awful and ugly he felt.

And then he told me this: "No matter how bad you feel, remember: *it will pass*. And things will get better. You've got to realize that the way you see yourself is what matters most. You can't get caught up in how other folks see you. You've got to be confident. You've got to be okay with who you are, son." He paused and smiled at me before continuing. "If I hadn't been rejected by that girl in high school, then it's possible I never would've married your mom. By rejecting me, she did me a huge favor." He leaned in and put his arm on my shoulder. "You too," he said, winking.

I smiled at him, and it was probably the first sincere smile I'd mustered in weeks.

"Now"—he stood up from the bar stool and walked in front of me—"how does the old man look?"

He took a few steps back and straightened his tie and smoothed his sleeves. Then he opened up his black suit jacket to reveal his red-and-black-striped suspenders. He adjusted his pocket square and pushed up his eyeglasses. He was modeling for me.

"You look sharp, Daddy."

"Well, thank ya!" he said with a smile.

Moments later, Mom came down the stairs. She looked gorgeous, wearing a black dress and black heels, carrying a white clutch purse. The shimmer of her dress highlighted the silver streaks in her hair. Her eyes met Dad's, and for the first time, I saw my parents not only as my parents, but also as two people very much in love with one another.

"Hey, good-looking!" Mom exclaimed to Dad.

Playfully, he looked around the room before offering with a smile, "You talking to *me*?!"

Mom took Dad's arm and away they went. I thought about

how confident Dad looked, how easy and charming he was. I thought about how beautiful Mom looked and how lovingly she gazed at him.

Maybe there was a time when Dad didn't like his reflection either, I thought. *I'll be okay.*

After they left, Dad's words echoed, playing over again in my head like a tape loop: *You've got to be okay with who you are, son.* It became clear to me that seeing myself as beautiful through my own eyes was more important than being seen as beautiful through the gaze of others. This was the lesson. I got up and walked to the bathroom, stood at the sink, and confronted my reflection. My journey toward self-acceptance began in that mirror, when I saw myself—for the very first time—as a young man.

 Nate Smith is a drummer who has played with bassist Dave Holland, saxophonists Chris Potter and Ravi Coltrane, and singers Patricia Barber, Somi, and José James.

A WOMAN'S PLACE IS IN THE KITCHEN

By Maneet Chauhan

"How old are you, madam?" That was one of the questions I was greeted with when I was doing my externship in India. I replied with a naïve pride, "I am seventeen years old, about to turn eighteen!" The chef who had asked me the question responded with shock. "Aren't your parents concerned about you?!" What he was really saying was: *How can they let a girl work in a hotel? In the kitchen? Shouldn't they be marrying you off right about now?*

This experience largely sums up the mentality of the Indian population in the late 1990s. I was the only girl in a kitchen of fifty to sixty men. I spent more time trying to convince people that what I was doing was not a hobby than I did actually cooking. It wasn't me trying to rebel against my parents. It was not me trying to learn how to cook so that I could create delicious hotel-style dishes for my husband. This was my dream. It was my life's goal, my ambition, my profession. It was my career and something I was planning to do for the rest of my life. This was one of the many sexist encounters I was subjected to in the kitchens in India.

There were many other remarks, but I think I had developed such a thick skin by then that I just naturally responded with a cheeky comment and in turn was labeled too smart for my own good. Call it a no-win situation. But who is laughing now?

Growing up female in India is paradoxical. The country has cultivated some of the most powerful women in history—a prime minister, a president, freedom fighters, and so many other accomplished and talented women. We are taught about inspirational women throughout our schooling. Indian culture perpetually praises goddesses, yet girls are considered burdens. I was very fortunate to grow up in a more progressive family. Despite being born into a society in which boys were more desirable, my sister and I were never faced with limitations at home. We were never told we could not do something because we were girls. Quite the contrary—we were told, "You are girls, so you can do anything!" However, that was not the environment outside our house.

I remember an interaction my mom had when we were traveling by train to visit our grandparents. A lady—ironically enough—turned to my mom and asked, "How many children do you have?" My mom pointed to the two of us, and the lady responded, "No, I mean how many children . . . how many boys?" Quizzically, my mom looked at the lady and said, "What are these, cattle?!" Unfortunately, most of the time, it's a woman saying these words. It's hard to fathom now that just a few decades ago, when a girl was born—if she was allowed to be born or live at all—society viewed it as a curse instead of encouraging the young, brilliant mind. Instead of letting the girl blossom, the narrow-minded society was adamant about crushing that blossom. These remarks were spoken so flippantly; people assumed girls were supposed to hear them and accept them. When I was born, my mom's aunt said to her, "What?! You gave birth to another girl?"

Walking home from school was a pretty dreadful experience. As we hit adolescence, we girls would rush home, usually in large groups, like herds of sheep. Heaven forbid we were alone; that would open us up to the boys who would go by on their bicycles, trying to grope us—which we were trained not to speak about. What gave those boys that right? What made them think that they could invade our space? Imagine being an adolescent girl in an environment like that. Imagine walking down the street and being subjected to catcalls and lewd comments about your gender, about your body, about how you walk, about how you talk. And we were supposed to just keep quiet, look down, keep walking. We felt like it was our fault, like we had done something wrong. This was simply the norm in Indian culture. We spent all our time thinking about how *not* to stand out, how to blend in with our surroundings so as not to call attention to ourselves. Can you imagine growing up in that environment?

But back inside my home, it was not this way. I have such fond memories of my dad and what he taught me as I grew up. He used to regularly address large crowds at conferences. He had so much confidence, and he told me to learn to pretend—act like you are not afraid, and over time you will no longer be afraid! I learned how to do just that. There are moments even today when I have to walk onto a stage and I catch my breath. I start acting like I am not nervous, and then it goes away. How does one become confident? That's a loaded question. It is our responsibility as women to nurture the girls in our lives, along with the boys. We must encourage them and ensure they know that they can do anything they put their minds to.

It is okay to fail, and you will come across tough times—after all, that is what life is all about. Having the right attitude is paramount to success. So know that anything is possible because strength comes from within yourself. Don't look to others for strength and validation. Decide what you want to achieve and be determined to achieve those goals. No ambition is too big and no dream is unattainable as long as you believe in yourself! When adversity comes your way, you do not succumb to it. You learn from it, you become stronger. The only thing you have complete control over in life is you. It's up to you to create your own story. Go out and show the world you are a force to be reckoned with!

 Maneet Chauhan is a James Beard Foundation Award recipient, the chef and owner of Chauhan Ale & Masala House in Nashville, and a judge on Food Network's Chopped.

BE BIGGER THAN YOUR STORY

A Conversation with
Tay Anderson and Leland Melvin

Leland: Tay, my name is Leland Melvin, and I'm a former NFL player and astronaut who has had a chance to see our planet from an incredible vantage point: space. I saw how we could work together as a team off the planet, and in some cases even with countries that used to be at war with each other. I heard about your incredible story and wanted to talk to you to find out how more students can be inspired to effect positive change.

Tay: My name's Tay Anderson, and I am currently a freshman at Metropolitan State University of Denver. And I'm also the youngest person in the history of Colorado to run for office. I ran for the Denver school board in November 2017. I didn't win, but it was a close race among three candidates, and I learned a lot during the campaign.

Leland: Why did you run for the school board?

Tay: I ran because I'm a student who's been homeless, who's been in and out of foster care, and really there's never been anybody from the district who's been in my corner to advocate for me. So I ran to give back to the students of Denver, to let them know that since I didn't have a champion, I'm going to fight to *be* their champion. I also ran just to bring more accountability and transparency to our board and our budget, because we've been spending a lot of money on the administrative side, but we haven't been giving a lot of money to our students and our classrooms. And our teachers need a raise.

Leland: Okay. And tell me a little bit about your upbringing.

Tay: I was raised by my grandmother in Kansas City. I never met my father, and my mother and I have always had a rocky relationship. And so my grandmother has been the backbone of my life. She was an educator for over thirty-five years, and she's just kind of my everything. She's battling cancer in Kansas right now, so I don't always get to see her. But I was raised in a very Christian household. I moved out to Denver with my mother my freshman year of high school, and we didn't have the best of relationships, so then I ended up going in and out of foster care. Eventually I became homeless. And so I just kind of started from the bottom and tried to move my way up to the top.

Leland: When I went through challenges, like losing my hearing in a training accident, it was my faith that got me through some of the toughest times. Does your faith keep you grounded and give you the hope to move forward?

Tay: Yes. My grandmother has always taught me, no matter what, to keep God in the forefront of my life. And so that's what I continue to do. Continue to be a man in God. Continue to never give up, because when so many people try to knock me for running for office because of my age, I hit those who utilize biblical stances with, "Well, Jesus was twelve and he was preaching."

Leland: [*Laughs.*] Right.

Tay: So you can't tell me it's not possible for young people to start leading, because Jesus was leading when he was young. Whether he was the Messiah or not, he was still leading. And so that's something I continue to let people know—that you can't knock young people for that. And I've always kept my faith at the forefront, but I've never used my faith to dictate policies.

Leland: And who or what inspires you the most?

Tay: *Who* would probably be President Obama. He was told by so many that he could not make it. And that there was no way a black man would be elected president. And he was like, "Just believe me. Just watch this." And he defied the odds. He won the nomination against a former First Lady and US senator. And then he went on to beat another fellow senator for the presidency, and became a successful president, in my opinion. He served two terms and he did great things for the American people. His never-giving-up spirit continues to drive me. And his farewell speech in January, when he was speaking to young people about getting involved, really resonated with me. That right there is it. I've heard Hillary Clinton say it. I've heard Bernie Sanders say it. I've heard Barack Obama say it. These three people have different views on the country and they've all said unanimously, "Young people, get involved." And that's why I did this.

Leland: Let's fast-forward twenty years. It's 2038. I see humans living and working together in orbit around Mars by that time. What do you see this world looking like in twenty years?

Tay: I see it with a President Tay Anderson! I might be finishing my first year in office. But I really am concerned about what our future is going to be because of the current administration in the White House dismantling every single thing that is going well for us without offering any alternatives. How do we come up with a way to fix it that pleases both sides? That's one of the biggest things to remember: When you assume the office of the presidency, you're not the president of the Republican Party. You're not the president of the Democratic Party. You're the president of the American people, and our commander in chief, and those who are in office need to act like it. So I fear that in twenty years we're going to be in conflict with other countries. I would really love to see the United States sit down at the table with these world leaders, with people we might not see eye to eye with, and come to a compromise about how we best move forward. We all want to see our countries prosper. We want to see our people happy, living free. But how do we do that? Divisiveness is not getting us there. Kim Jong Un saying he wants to nuke us every week and Trump tweeting that he's going to do something back is not getting us there. The country is going to be in a rebuilding phase, because this administration is going to have a heavy impact on the next several presidents we have. And so that's my biggest fear. That if this dude gets elected for a second term, how do we as the American people come together and let him know that he is the president for *all* Americans, not just those who elected him? How do we move forward as the people? Because that's who I represent. I don't represent a party. I would love to be sitting down having this conversation in twenty years, telling Republicans, "I know you probably didn't elect me as your president, but I want to make sure that your voices are heard and that you have seats at the table as well."

Leland: Do you think that most students around your age, whether they're Democrat or Republican or independent, feel the same way that you do?

Tay: I would say that the Democrat students feel that Trump is just evil and he needs to go, and I would say that he needs to go, too. I think that the Republican students would praise him and say that he's doing a great job. But I think the one thing that we all bring to the table and that we all agree on is that we need a president who represents both sides. We need a president who hears both sides of the aisle and not just what he or she wants to hear. Or *they*, if we ever have a nonbinary president. We need to make sure that the president understands what it means to take the oath of office to become the commander in chief of the nation. It's bigger than just saying, "I'm president now. It's my way or the highway." That's where young people get together and say that we need a president who represents all of us.

Leland: I asked you about inspiration. So twenty years out, you run for president of the United States of America and you win. You have your two terms. What do you want to do after that?

Tay: First of all, I'm going to do what President Obama did and take that nine months to myself. But I'm going to come back to give back to young people. Young people are my passion. They are always going to be in the forefront of my life. So I've already decided that I'm getting an organization together, a 501(c)(4) called Why Wait?, to train young people to run for office and get them the tools to let them know that they can do it. And I want to donate a lot of money. I will donate directly to schools and cities that need it the most.

Leland: Do you know if there are a lot of students who are homeless and still in school?

Tay: We don't know exactly how many students are homeless, but we do know that about two-thirds of Denver's 92,000 students qualify for subsidized lunches, which is a proxy for poverty.

Leland: And do the schools do anything to reach out to those students? Do they even know that some of those students are homeless?

Tay: Some of them do. They put me in a youth program that gives gift cards and hygiene stuff and takes care of basic needs for individual students who claim independence and do not have parents at home.

Leland: And I know that this is a problem not just in Denver or Colorado, but around the world. You know, we as a group of leaders have to make sure that we take care of all people. I'll definitely be voting for you for president if I'm still around—I like your focus on ensuring that we take care of the marginalized, the disaffected. And that's something that we must do. Do you have a favorite quote or scripture?

Tay: This is the scripture I want to be remembered by. It's 2 Timothy 4:7–8: "I have fought the good fight, I have finished the race, I have kept the faith. Now there is in store for me the crown of righteousness, which the Lord, the righteous Judge, will award to me on that day—and not only to me, but also to all who have longed for his appearing." It's basically saying, Tay was always told he could not do it, but he did it. He fought a good fight, he ran a good race, and he always kept the faith. And it was not about him, but about every single individual who said he could not make it, and about defying the odds and paving the way for young people to see they can be anything that they want to be.

Leland: Right. That's a great scripture. Fighting a good fight and running a good race. And that doing that is enough. Anything else that you want to add?

Tay: I would just say to continue to lift young people up in your community. Tell young people to continue to strive. I had so many teachers tell me, "You'll never make it out. You'll never graduate." Well, I graduated. Or "You'll never do anything with your life." Well, I received 25 percent of the vote for the position of a director for the school district, which means I came pretty close to becoming one of their bosses.

Leland: Why did they tell you that? What was the thing that made them want to say that to you?

Tay: I wasn't a perfect student. I always slacked off. I messed up my freshman year severely. And I had several teachers who said, "Well, we're here whether you succeed or you fail. We still get paychecks either way." And I had teachers say that I'd never make it out. I also had family members say that. So it's about proving them wrong and showing the world that it can tell me I'll never amount to anything, but I'll come out on top. Because I know my worth.

Leland: And that grit, determination, going against the odds and going against what people have told you—is that the thing that really keeps you pushing forward to find a better place for yourself and for others?

Tay: Yes. I have never met my father, and that makes me work ten times harder to provide my future family with a better life than I was given. Because I never want my future kids to say that I wasn't there. And my backup plan instead of being a politician is to be a teacher. So I will continue to fight for them and continue to make sure that my future family knows that I'll always be there for them, that I'm not going to be another statistic. The statistic says one in three black men goes to jail, but I want to change that statistic and say three out of three black men gets accepted to college.

Leland: I'm with you, brother. Well, Tay, I'm so proud of you and I appreciate everything that you're doing. I love your strength, your grit, your grace, your faith. And I believe in you. I believe that you are what this planet needs: a person who came from hard and humble beginnings and has never given up on trying to make this world a better place, not just for himself but for others. Your can-do spirit and positive attitude are infectious. Keep the faith, my brother.

Auontai "Tay" Anderson, nineteen, a former candidate for the Denver Public Schools Board of Education, was, at eighteen, the youngest person to run for public office in Colorado.

Leland Melvin is a former astronaut and NFL player, an educator, a photographer, and a musician.

TWISTED-MOUTH

By Jeff Gomez

I had been on the streets alone for days. Skinny and exhausted, I needed cash. The older dudes down Times Square told me that if I was too pussy to rob people, I could dance for money. I had the body for it. At seventeen, I was underage, but that made it better. So I went, but once I got into the club, I never got a chance to ask for a job. A customer there offered me a better one. "You don't have to do anything. Just stand in front of me in my room," he said. Then he laid his big, meaty hand on my chest. "You're beautiful."

The hotel was a dive near Penn Station on Eighth Avenue. I was sitting on the edge of the bed with my leather jacket still on. Next to me on the threadbare blanket was a crumpled twenty-dollar bill. It was the summer of 1980, hot as hell. My T-shirt was soaked with sweat. Sirens, rap music, and shouting in Spanish came in through the open window. He was in the bathroom, sink running as he coughed up giant wads of phlegm. Soon, to keep that money, I'd have to take off my clothes and let him play with himself in front of me.

My brain was frying with a million thoughts, none of them good. Awful images misfiring, repeating themselves into infinity. I touched my fingers to my lips, trying to comprehend what had led me to this place. Most of all, I thought about how this man was a liar. Nothing beautiful here . . .

. . .

The second I was born, there were already three strikes against me. The first was that I was homeless. My mom had just turned fifteen, and nice young Jewish girls from Alphabet City did not get pregnant by Latin boys from the Baruch projects across Houston Street. Her parents kicked her out of their tenement apartment, and she was living in a women's shelter on Staten Island when she had me.

Strike two was that the doctor who delivered me, he squeezed too hard on the forceps—these big metal tongs that he used to pull my big head out of my tiny mother—and he damaged my seventh cranial nerve, paralyzing the left side of my face and forever giving me my crooked smile.

Strike three was my last name, which my mom gave me long before she eventually married my dad—Gomez. In the New York City of the early 1960s, Puerto Ricans competed with black people at the bottom of society's barrel, and they often came up short. Third swing and a miss. Little Donny Gomez was out before he even got started.

A few days after I showed up, a social worker with the hint of a beating heart came to my mom and leveled with her. A turned-out teen with a kid and no husband didn't have much of a future. It was going to be bad for them both. Why not put Donny into foster care, at least until Mom finished high school? There was a family upstate, Irish, a good one, willing to take the baby in.

What usually happened was that those babies disappeared into the system forever, their mothers never able to get back on their feet, never able to retrieve them. But when my mom signed the papers, she looked at my bruised face and my weird, twisted sneer, and she swore to herself that she'd get me back. For better or worse, she was good to her word.

I would spend my next thirty months in a pretty good place. They were the Mangels family. Suburban New Rochelle, New York. House with a white picket fence. Fresh-faced brothers and sisters with names like Bobby and Nancy. A dog named Chipper. My foster mom had round, rosy cheeks and was always smiling. They changed my name from Donny to Jeffrey, and embraced me and loved me like I was theirs.

The Mangelses quickly realized I was an endlessly curious kid, and they indulged me. They'd let me study every ornament on the Christmas tree for hours. Their backyard was my kingdom. I was reading *Where the Wild Things Are* before my third birthday. Once every several months, a pretty golden-haired girl—my birth mom, but she called herself Estelle—would come take me down to the city, and in Central Park I would press my ear to her wristwatch and listen for long moments to its soft ticking.

In those years, Estelle worked hard and was set to graduate from Mabel Dean Bacon Vocational High School with some mad typing skills. At seventeen, she screwed up her courage and went and found Joe Gomez on the benches in front of a building on Baruch Drive. She told him they were going up to New Rochelle to get their kid, and then they were going to get married. My mom was a pistol, and something in her eyes told Joe not to argue with her.

Mrs. Mangels was heartbroken. "If you take Jeffrey, his life will be hard," she told Estelle. "If we keep him, he'll grow up in a nice place. We'll send him to college. He'll be happy." But Mom was determined, and so I left to go down to the city with the pretty blond girl and her scary dark-skinned friend, and I'd never, ever return.

My mom and I moved into my dad's parents' house in Jamaica, Queens. Suddenly everyone was speaking in a language I didn't understand. It sounded like yelling, a lot of it directed at me. They grabbed my head and demanded to know, "Why is his mouth like that?" Rather than calling me, they pulled me roughly by an arm or leg. They washed me in the sink instead of the bathtub.

One morning I was startled by a cockroach crawling up the kitchen wall. A man—he lived there, but I didn't know him—smiled at me, then used his newspaper to swipe the roach onto me. The fear that had been building up inside burst into hysteria. I completely lost it and ran screaming through the house. My mom had left for work, and the rest of the family rushed to see what had happened. When I told them, they shouted at me, glaring down with utter disdain:

Of course he screams like a little girl, look at his long hair. Look how he spends all his time reading books. Look at how his judía *mother coddles him. He is* flojo. *Weak. Like a girl.*

That cut it. Time to go home. Back to Bobby and Nancy and Chipper. Back to my mommy, Mrs. Mangels. But I could not convince Estelle. She was sweet and kind, and great at using stuffed toys and puppets to distract me, but there would be no train to New Rochelle for me.

So I went to war. I cried, screamed, and threw tantrums. I hid and shat my pants. One day I found a hammer and pounded it on a coffee table, leaving welts in the wood. Out of nowhere, Joe, the scary man, came up to me, pulled the belt from his waist, coiled it around his fist, and lashed it across my legs and ass.

At three, I'd never felt such pain. It had to be an accident. I'd been threatened a number of times, but not hit. But his rage was unmistakable. He meant it. He raised the belt, daring me to talk back to him. I fell silent. Soon I learned to stay that way. I would never get used to the belt.

A year or two later, my mom and my dad and my new baby sister and I moved out of Jamaica, back to the Baruch projects in Manhattan. It had gotten much worse there. Teenagers wore gang colors, smashing windows out of half-abandoned tenements. Drug addicts shot up in our stairwells. Garbage and burned-up cars littered the streets. The Vietnam War, police corruption, and political assassinations were everywhere in the news.

Some of the kids in the neighborhood, they looked at me—with my welfare glasses and my long hair and my permanent smirk—like I was from outer space. And back then you did not welcome creatures from the stars. You jeered at them, called them "twisted-mouth," punched them as hard as you could.

Through tears one night I asked my mom, "Why do so many people make fun of me? What am I doing to make them hate me?" Seated on my bed in the dark, she took a drag of her Marlboro, and I watched the tip of the cigarette glow bright orange.

"Find it in your heart to forgive them, Jeffrey. They don't understand how special you are, because they're just not smart. One day we'll get out of this place, and you'll find smart people, and they'll love you."

I never forgot those words. About a year later, I finally started to understand them. We were over at a neighbor's apartment, and I was watching TV in the living room with some kids my age. It was a new show called *The Brady Bunch,* a sitcom about a blended family with six children. They seemed to genuinely love each other, and when the kids made mistakes or did something wrong, the parents would calmly talk to them and they'd solve the problem together. *Pow!*

One of the older kids, Gordon, smacked me in the head. "Hey, Jeffrey! Those white-boy faggots talk just like you!" He rolled on the floor with laughter, but I just stared at the screen. The dude was right. Somehow I was like these people, these Bradys. It was as if I'd lived another life and suddenly dimly remembered it. To me the show wasn't some goofy Hollywood fantasy—it was an affirmation, proof positive, that the world I was living in was not the only world.

In that moment, I felt both yearning and a deep sorrow. I was still missing puzzle pieces, but for the first time I saw their shapes. In the days that followed, I also felt a strange, growing certainty that it didn't have to be this way.

Maybe there was more to these sitcoms and cartoons, these comics and chapter books, these Motown songs and these movies down at the Loew's Delancey, than bright colors and splashy action. If I could glimpse this other life in these stories, then maybe somewhere inside them there were clues that would lead me back to it. But that road was perilous, and at night there would be monsters along the way.

Mom got my sis and me out of the projects in 1972, and into an apartment on the Long Island Expressway in Flushing, Queens. I should have been happy, and in a sense I was. I loved stories and was reading everything from the Holy Bible to *Fear of Flying.* I loved Tolkien most of all and would lose myself to the great War of the Ring in the backwoods of Kissena Park until it was too dark to read the words.

But as I got older, the injuries I'd suffered and stifled took hold and started echoing endlessly in the recesses of my mind. I worried about nonsense, checking door and window latches even though I knew they were locked. I became obsessed with the shape of my body and deprived myself of food for days. Images of blades and blood would flood my thoughts for no apparent reason. In high school, these waking nightmares would rush out of nowhere behind my eyes, hitting me so hard I would grasp the sides of my desk until my knuckles turned white.

By seventeen I was cutting myself to try to chase away these demented fantasies, laying nicks and slits low across my abs, where no one could see. My mom sensed something was wrong and kept asking questions, but I was too ashamed to answer. That pissed both of us off. We fought. I left the house and would live on the streets for days at a time.

· · ·

Why am I here? Do I need the money that badly? Am I even gay? The heavyset man came out of the bathroom and lumbered toward me. He opened a small, brightly colored bottle, amyl nitrate, and hunched over for a second to loudly inhale its contents. "Have some. It'll make it easier from behind. Take off your jacket." *Idiot! Did you really think he just wanted you to pose for him? For twenty bucks, he's going to want a lot more.*

I couldn't move, even though it felt like an animal was alive and panicking in my chest. But then, even though I was awash in darkness and hunger and gore—burning to be anything other than what I was—something clicked deep inside. I heard a vital reminder in the voices of my heroes, from Jesus to Shaft to Mr. Spock. They were absolute in their conviction: *It doesn't have to be this way.*

I stood up suddenly and glared at the startled john. Then I made for the door, the crumpled twenty still on the bed. "Weirdo!" he bellowed behind me. "What's wrong with you?" Outside, choking back tears, I started running. I ran like hellhounds were at my heels. I guess they were.

The road I was on could have ended with me as an addict or a prostitute, or dead of AIDS. *Story* saved me. In stories, I found codes that I somehow learned to decipher, even at the darkest, loneliest moments of my life. I found values in those codes: the courage to push back against overwhelming opposition, to believe in my heart that I could somehow reach the next rung on the ladder; the self-worth and resilience and ambition and will to rail against impossible odds. Solving those story codes would reveal for me a path out of paralyzing anxiety. They would become my map to success.

As a child, I somehow figured that if somewhere the sunshine world of *The Brady Bunch* was real, then maybe behaving a bit like a Brady would get me one step closer to it. Later I realized that if I could ride the *Enterprise* with Kirk and Spock, then I could take home passion and logic. I could stalk the moors of the British countryside with Sherlock Holmes and bring back deductive reasoning. I could walk the Shire with Gandalf the Grey and realize that even in the darkest of times, "all we have to decide is what to do with the time that is given us."

In the years to come, I'd become something of an expert in story, and in how stories can be woven across comic books and video games, films and the internet. In doing so, I got to travel the world, create vast fantasy and science-fiction sagas, work on a movie set with James Cameron, finally meet those smart people my mom promised me.

But I also forgave and never forgot those kids I left behind in the projects. I think about them every day while I do my work. I hope that some of them will crack the codes that I weave into these story worlds. I hope they'll realize that there are other ways to be, free of violence and despair. And that from these stories they can build ladders, and climb up and out of everything they know to find a better place. Even if they're scared and scarred, lost in a merciless city. Even if there are already three strikes against them.

 Jeff Gomez is a producer who has worked on Pirates of the Caribbean, Avatar, Halo, *and* Men in Black *and is the founder of Starlight Runner Entertainment.*

THE UNFINISHED
MAULIK PANCHOLY PILOT

By Maulik Pancholy

FADE IN:

EXT. GOOD SAMARITAN HOSPITAL—JANUARY 18, 1974

The camera hovers high up in the sky, looking over the moonlit town of Dayton, Ohio. Suddenly we hear a baby cry. Like, really cry. Like an *Oh my gah! I just got born! What is happening?!* kind of cry. Our camera flies down from the sky and through the roof of the hospital, races along the halls, and lands on BABY MAULIK craning his tiny little neck to look at all the other babies in the nursery.

> BABY MAULIK
> (in his mind, obviously; he's just a baby)
> Whoa. Wait a minute! Am I the only Indian baby in here?

He rolls his head to the other side. It's not easy. I mean, he doesn't even have fully developed neck muscles yet.

BABY MAULIK (CONT'D)
(still in his mind . . . this *is* reality, after all,
people)
Oh, wait. Is that . . . ? Nope. She's not Indian
either! Hold the phone—why does nobody look
like me?

Ominous footsteps. NURSE FREDDIE's enormous face
pops into frame: a tangled wasp's nest of blond hair, and
spiderwebs of mascara surrounding her eyes.

BABY MAULIK
(frantic)
W-w-what do you want? Who are you?

NURSE FREDDIE
I think you know what I want.

BABY MAULIK
How did you hear me?! I don't even know how
to talk out loud yet!

NURSE FREDDIE
(ignoring him)
Do you know what happens down here to little
babies who are *different*?
(singsongy and menacing)
One of these things is not like the others. . . .

She lets out an evil laugh and starts to reach for him.

BABY MAULIK
(scrunching up his little baby face)
What the what, lady?!

NURSE FREDDIE

Oh, I'll show you what the what!

BABY MAULIK
(sarcastic)

Um, yeah, okay, *real* original. Way to say *exactly* what I just said right back to me. Is that all you got?

NURSE FREDDIE
(thrown)

Wha—?

BABY MAULIK

You're going to have to do better than that, nurse lady!

Baby Maulik balls up his little baby fists and starts punching the air like a madman.

BABY MAULIK (CONT'D)

Nobody puts Baby Maulik in a corner!

Okay, okay, okay. That's not *exactly* how the first day of my life went. But there are parts of it that aren't totally off base. I *was* born in Dayton, Ohio, in 1974. In the 1970s there were fewer than twenty thousand Asian American people in the entire state of Ohio. You can google it. That's not a lot of Asian American people, which means even fewer Indian American people. So there weren't a lot of other babies who looked like me.

So maybe I wasn't battling evil nurses, but I did have a sense very early on that I was different. That wasn't limited just to my skin color. I used to write my 4s backward; when my parents would try to correct me, I'd say, "Well, that's *my* four, and that's *your* four!" So I guess I was kind of sassy. I was also really scrawny; when I was five, I had to take all these tests to figure out why I was so little. A doctor had me run up and down stairs, jump on boxes, and do all sorts of physical challenges. Turned out everything was fine (take that, staircase!), but I wouldn't catch up to the other kids for a few years. Instead of playing sports, I wanted to tap-dance, which wasn't exactly considered cool at the time. Things like math came pretty easy to me, so I was definitely a "nerd" at school.

And I loved acting. I loved make-believe and playing characters. My cousins and I would put on shows for our parents at family gatherings (and charge them admission!). Cartoons, television shows, movies, and plays mesmerized me. I loved *storytelling*. Acting. I wanted to be an actor. I wanted it so badly that I told my parents (in between correcting their *very* weird 4s) when I was only five years old that I was going to be an actor.

That seemed perfectly reasonable: do what you love. But the thing is, I never saw anyone who looked like me on TV or in the movies. All my favorite cartoon characters (the Super Friends, Scooby-Doo) were either white or . . . well, dogs. There were virtually no brown people on the television shows we watched (or the shows my parents tried to *keep* us from watching, like *Dallas* and *Falcon Crest*), and the occasional Indian person who popped up in a film was laughable, stereotypical, and often played by a white actor in brownface (*Short Circuit,* anyone?). So what kind of career was *I* going to have?

You might call that lack of representation subtle messaging that brown people don't belong. That our stories aren't worth telling, that we're not actually a part of the fabric of American culture.

Other times the message was not so subtle. I remember my

mom getting rear-ended when I was a teenager. It was clearly the other driver's fault, but as my mom got out of the car, he yelled, "You're not even from here! Why don't you just go back to your own country?" I remember sitting in the car, anger coursing through my veins, but also fear. Someone was trying to intimidate us because we were Indian.

That same feeling of fear crept in when I realized I was gay. Not only was it terrifying to think that the people I cared about might not accept me, but there was also the glaring fact that there were hardly any gay characters on television, let alone openly gay actors. Did this mean I would have to live a life of hiding in order to be successful?

In the beginning, I did hide. I tried to be just like everyone else. When I was in college, it was pretty easy to forget that I wasn't white. I was immersed in an excellent theater program where we studied great playwrights like Ibsen, Chekhov, Brecht, and Shakespeare. All amazing, but for the most part all white. Theirs were the parts I got to play in class, and I just assumed that meant I'd get to play any parts I wanted to when I graduated.

When I moved to Los Angeles shortly after college, however, I realized that I couldn't actually hide being brown. The parts I thought would be open to me were in fact reserved for actors who were . . . well, *not* brown. I was thrilled when I landed my first guest-starring role on a television show, but horrified that I'd be playing a foreign exchange student who wore a turban, ate camel nuggets, spoke in a heavy accent, and was basically the butt of every joke. That wasn't what I had imagined when I said I wanted to be an actor.

Around this time, I also started to come to terms with my sexuality. While I began to talk to friends and family, I was still terrified about what this would mean in the entertainment industry. But I also knew that there had to be more than a life of running away from myself and playing degrading roles. Somewhere inside me was, after all, that kid who was so certain of himself, who knew a backward *4* was *his* 4! I wasn't going to give up.

I continued taking classes, showing up to auditions, and working to be the best actor I could be. I got accepted to the Yale School of Drama, and it was there that I started to profoundly understand that being an actor meant being willing to let my *true self* be a part of my work. Shortly after school, I started to land roles that were fulfilling.

On the Showtime series *Weeds,* I played Sanjay, a college tutor and drug dealer who came out as gay. He was both Indian American and a three-dimensional character, and I think it meant a great deal to Asian Americans, and to LGBTQ Asian Americans, to be represented on TV. On NBC's *30 Rock,* I played executive assistant Jonathan. I went toe to toe with comedy heavyweights Alec Baldwin and Tina Fey. This time, we weren't really concerned with the character's race; rather, the show explored the relationship between an executive assistant and his boss.

Being able to do this on television—getting to show that brown people are an integral part of American culture and not just a joke, and that LGBTQ characters can be represented in meaningful ways—made me want to do more. Being a public figure gave me a platform. I started to speak at various Asian American and LGBTQ nonprofit organizations. I traveled to universities to address students about why we need diversity in the media. I learned that there was great power not only in telling stories on television but also in sharing my *own* story with others.

In 2014, this work led to President Obama appointing me to the President's Advisory Commission on Asian Americans and Pacific Islanders. During my time at the White House, I helped create an anti-bullying campaign geared toward Asian American and Pacific

Islander kids called #ActToChange, which I continue to lead today. No one should feel that their differences make them less than.

The battle is far from over. I was the voice of Sanjay on the Nickelodeon cartoon *Sanjay and Craig*. I think of myself watching cartoons on weekend mornings and longing to see a character that looked like me; now I've given that to other kids. Sanjay was half-Indian and half-Caucasian, and just a regular kid who loved getting into gross stuff and going on crazy adventures. So many biracial and Asian American kids wrote to say how meaningful the character was to them. But there was also a writer who said in an interview that the show was "awkward" because "there's actually no reason for that character to be Indian"; he asked, "Why make [him] Indian?" He just didn't get it. So the fight goes on.

And the fight is big. There are a lot of people out there right now screaming, "Go back to your own country!" just like that guy yelled at my mom and me so many years ago. So I use acting and entertainment, and also social work and politics, to keep pushing back. This *is* my country.

For me, our strongest weapon is to keep telling our stories.

Which reminds me, I need to get back to the Unfinished Maulik Pancholy Pilot. That opening scene needs work. Scary nurses? Talking babies? *Really?* I do have an idea for the ending, though. I'm thinking:

ADULT MAULIK

Nevertheless, I persisted.

Maulik Pancholy is an actor best known for his work on 30 Rock, Weeds, Phineas and Ferb, *and* Sanjay and Craig.

YOU, SAILOR

By Erin McKeown

What is it to persist? Is it to be in the center of a swirling storm and still know you will navigate to safety? Or is it to look back on a voyage and, with perspective, appreciate the obstacles that presented themselves and were persisted over? When do we name ourselves *persistent*? Mine isn't a story about a flashy kind of triumph. It's a story about a quieter but no less important victory. Personal fears and family expectations could have shaped me, but it now seems inevitable: I was meant to live a creative life.

Living. That's what persistence feels like when you're in it. An explorer in uncharted waters who wants nothing more than to survive the next wave and see what lies on the other side. You'd never think of doing otherwise while it is happening. But looking back, you can see that sailing was actually persisting. In the same way, I was born to be a sailor, though it took me some time to recognize it.

> *no longer will i beneath you shelter*
> *all that you have given to me*
> *it was never on my behalf*

I grew up in a small town in Virginia. My parents had ordinary, respectable jobs—an engineer, a teacher. Education and good behavior were prized above all in our house. As was the middle-class norm of being *well rounded*. You should never be too much of any one thing. Not too loud or meek, athletic or artsy. You should know some history (though not be an expert), play some music (but just for experience), be able to make small talk at a party so as to have people remember you well. A little of it all, at a modest level, made one a *nice* person. Later I would come to see this idea as superficial and limiting, keeping me from diving deep into any one interest and overly worried by what others might think of me.

If you had asked ten-year-old me, *What do you want to be when you grow up?* I probably would have said something appropriate, at least to the adults I saw daily. I didn't know that you could be a sailor. I did know that I was curious, mechanical, good at tests. I liked sports and played plenty of them. But I also wrote books of poems and short stories and built functioning weather stations and elaborate forts in the backyard.

This led me, when I was eleven, to a summer camp in the Shenandoah Valley—a magical place where we learned about all kinds of topics in biology, did experiments, and wrote reports. But we also did kid-at-camp things like kiss on hikes down by the creek, compare secondary sex characteristics, and sing folk songs at night. Though I had been taking piano lessons since I was four, camp was the first place I ever saw anyone play the guitar, up close and right next to me while I sang along. Something inside me shifted.

After that first summer, I came home and knew I had to get a guitar and learn. I haunted the musical instruction section of my local library. I attached a piece of cardboard onto the handle of my tennis racket and carefully glued six pieces of yarn across it so I could practice chord fingerings. I think this was the beginning of my persistence. I began to smell the sea.

> what's this camaraderie of country
> that turns before me salty
> rust on fragile parts
> all this, all you have inspired
> the crew and ship of empire
> rig and mast and spars
> box of stripes and stars

Over the next several years, the guitar became all I thought about. It certainly threatened my potential for being *well rounded*. I took a few lessons, but the vast majority of my learning took place through jam sessions with friends, experiments on my four-track recorder, and eagle-eyed watching of my camp counselors' playing. I began to take my guitar with me to school, playing during lunch in the classrooms of supportive teachers. I never kept track of how much I played, I just played all the time I could. Incessant. Persistent.

Playing the guitar and writing songs (which I began to do immediately after learning basic chords) unlocked something inside me that I didn't know had been stuck. To *strum,* to *sing* moved molecules inside me that had been frozen in a respectable pose. Here was a place for my humor, for my longings, for my desire to take up more space. I know now that my guitar was a lifeboat, but at the time I just felt like I had untied a rope that had moored me. The only choice was to see what the next swell would bring.

The first time I was asked to perform with my guitar, I was struck with terror. Playing in front of an audience would simply be *too much*. I sensed it would go beyond *well rounded* and into the realm of something more fundamentally vulnerable. My true self, specific and strange, might be uncovered. I might be someone my audience did not like. I might do something embarrassing. Music would be no longer something to *dabble* in but something to swallow me whole if I surrendered to it. Like the ocean, I both longed for it and feared it.

I wish I could tell you how I made myself do that first performance, a shaky version of "The Rose" at a camp talent night when I was thirteen. But somehow my passion overcame my fear. I surrendered, and the pull of the sea carried me forward. I had begun to dream about a future in which performing wasn't so terrifying. I had started to lie in bed at night imagining being onstage and loving it, big gestures to huge crowds. While I listened to my worn-out Janis Joplin cassettes, I began to notice a few older women in town, two musicians and a painter who seemed to take up space in just the way I wanted to. They took an interest in me and told me stories of their own creative voyages. Part of persistence must be seeing others do the thing you want. Knowing it can be done. These women had built beautiful ships of their own design, flying under their own flags. I wanted the same for myself.

i am a king! you can't deny me my kingdom!

I'd like to say that after that first performance, everything was smooth sailing. But for years afterward I would be sick to my stomach anytime a performance approached. The only thing that has made it easier for me has been the thousands of times I have done it since. Perhaps another part of persistence is repetition. No matter what you are doing, the more you do it, the easier it becomes. I was practicing my knots, studying charts, and I was becoming a sailor.

I'd also like to say that I arrived fully formed as an artist, with unique things to say and a unique way of sounding. Also not true. For many years I sounded like my favorite musicians. Maybe not note for note, but in broad strokes I was imitating them. It seemed safer. It was definitely more comfortable. But then I began to grow uncomfortable with comparisons to other artists, with the shorthand that came from seeing a girl with an acoustic guitar in the late 1990s. Maybe that's part of persistence, too—recognizing where you chafe and heading toward it. It's very easy to sound like someone else; it is much harder to sound like yourself. I decided it was time to sound like myself.

> *you, sailor, on the lonely sea*
> *will you turn and promise me*
> *you'll always be alive*
> *oh, i might stutter, i might falter*
> *sail uncharted waters*
> *drowning, lost, then found*
> *drowning, lost, then found*

The painful part of this period was that I felt I had to step away from the artists who had nurtured me. These heroes who had offered something to me that I hadn't found at home, a safe harbor for my newly built ship while I got my bearings. My family at this time was suspicious of my choice to be an artist—perhaps they were trying to protect me from the failures that are so common in a creative life. Perhaps they simply didn't understand what it felt like to have to do something no matter what. Perhaps they didn't think going to sea a respectable choice. I do not come from a family of mariners.

But by this time I knew I was a sailor through and through. That there was no place for me but on the ocean. I knew that to truly come into myself as an artist and a person, I had to leave the shore of my family and the safe harbor of my heroes. I've since learned that they will always be there, in some capacity. That I can look back and there they'll be, hovering on the horizon or waving to me as we pass on our endless voyages.

It can be a lonely business, this persisting. People may fall by the wayside. You will outgrow relationships and geographies. But ultimately, there is a motor going inside you that drives you toward the discovery. Your gut will tell you, you will feel pulled, you will listen to that tug. And the rewards for this will be obvious: a chance to make some change in the world, the confidence of knowing you can accomplish whatever you set your mind to. But I wouldn't worry about perspective right now. I wouldn't worry about persisting. I would just keep sailing.

 Erin McKeown is a musician, writer, and producer known internationally for her prolific disregard of stylistic boundaries.

TRIPLE THREAT

A Conversation with
Tamika, Tauja, and Kenyon Catchings

Tauja: Basketball has always been a big part of our lives. Our dad, Harvey Catchings, was a professional basketball player, so between watching his games and practices and shooting hoops in the driveway, we were always actively engaged in the game of basketball.

Tamika: I was in third grade when I took up the sport in an organized fashion. Tauja and I were members of an all-boys team that our father coached for the park district in Deerfield, Illinois. In seventh grade I made my first goal of wanting to be in the NBA. I wanted a big goal, something to strive for, and following in my father's footsteps seemed like a real possibility. I already just loved the game so much.

Kenyon: I began playing basketball with any basket I could find. At school, at friends' houses . . . anywhere there was a hoop. I thought that I had a really good chance of making it to the NBA until I was in seventh or eighth grade. At that time, I started playing in tournaments across the Midwest and realized there were many players as good as or better than me. My parents always stressed the importance of education first and that we would not be able to do any extracurricular activities if we didn't do well in school.

Tauja: I think that we've always had a unique perspective on professional sports because of our dad. For many people it's unattainable as a career, but for us it was a reality. And a serious option.

Tamika: I didn't really think about what I would do if I didn't play basketball. But I always knew to have a backup plan. I knew that no matter what, I would love to do something around the game and growing it.

Kenyon: Outside of basketball, I envisioned myself doing something in either accounting or finance. Once I got to college, I quickly realized that even though I love numbers, I love interacting with people too much to deal mainly with numbers. That was when I learned about business marketing and my ability to develop relationships and connections with customers.

Tauja: In addition to teaching us how to play basketball, our dad always instilled in us an entrepreneurial spirit. From the time we were young, he'd give us a certain amount of money to start little businesses. From lemonade stands and babysitting clubs to "T&T's Treasures," we were taught the importance of having multiple streams of income and being our own bosses.

Tamika: I believed from the time I wrote it down on a school paper as a kid that I was going to be in the NBA. The WNBA didn't come till my freshman year of college, so I switched goals at that point. But when the women's national team blew up during the 1996 Olympics and I was participating on one of the Junior Olympic teams, my aspiration to be an Olympian was born. I wanted to follow in their footsteps, and my dad's.

Tauja: In college I realized I could compete and go further in my basketball career if I wanted to.

Tamika: My biggest obstacle as a teen was wanting so much at once. I was the one who set goals for everything, and I lived my life to reach those goals. I don't know if that's an obstacle or not, but there have been a few times as I've gotten older when adversity has hit, and because of the preparation from when I was younger, I've been able to push through. As far as off the court, I'd say my obstacles were just trying to fit in and be "normal." I was born with moderate hearing loss, and because I was unable to hear, I spoke with a speech impediment. Combine my hearing aids with glasses and braces, and I was a target for bullies. Basketball was always my escape from bullying. I may have been teased for being different, but I more than made up for it on the court. The game gave me the confidence that I lacked, and I poured my heart into it.

Kenyon: My biggest obstacle was my health. As a junior in high school, I was diagnosed with an intestinal disorder that sapped me of my strength and my ability to play basketball at a high level. It forced me to focus on school and apply to colleges as a regular student, not a member of the basketball team.

Tauja: Having a dad who played pro sports was a blessing and a curse! On one hand, he was able to coach and teach us. But on the other hand, he was pretty hard on us when it came to basketball. He really pushed us, sometimes too hard. It was toughest on his relationship with Tamika.

Tamika: Dad always pushed me, especially after I made my goal to be in the WNBA. He knew that the road wouldn't be easy, and he wanted me to always perform at my best. Even when I got to the pro level, he never backed off. Sometimes I wouldn't speak to him for months because of how the game and my success sometimes made him. If I had a bad game, I would hear all about it, but for the good games it would be just a simple text. Sometimes I dreaded picking up my phone to his text messages more than anything else.

I'd stopped wearing my hearing aids in elementary school to avoid teasing and questions and stares. My freshman year of college at Tennessee, Coach Pat Summitt sat me down and challenged me to get back into wearing them. She taught me to embrace my hearing loss and to start wearing my hearing aids, to use my platform as a way to empower others with disabilities. The way Pat could inspire people was absolutely amazing. She pushed all of us to look outside ourselves, and I'm so thankful that she did.

Kenyon: I fought through the illness my junior year, but when it recurred during my senior season I decided to focus on being a student, and went to college with the intention of taking one year off from playing basketball to get my health under control. By the end of that year, I realized that I loved basketball but no longer had the passion to do everything it takes to play at the collegiate level.

Tamika: Throughout everything, I wanted success, and the drive to achieve it was there. The obstacles were part of my journey to push me, but facing the adversity I did early on strengthened me in my faith and in helping others. There were so many people who helped me along my journey, and I hope to help others overcome their obstacles and push forward.

People always ask, if I could change anything about my journey, what would it be. My answer is: nothing. Every experience I've been through has shaped me, and everything I will go through will shape me, for my future and what God has planned for me next.

Kenyon: I was able to overcome obstacles by realizing that the plan for me was not to play collegiate or professional basketball. Once I realized that I would have to follow a different career path, I was able to develop a different skill set, and my focus became to be as successful as possible in the business world. My advice is to always follow your dreams, but have a backup plan. Set goals that will help you get closer to achieving your dreams, and always be willing to work harder than those around you.

Tauja: Play multiple sports and don't specialize in one sport until high school or later. We played everything from soccer to softball, volleyball, tennis, gymnastics, swimming, bowling— you name it, we probably played it. This helped us be more well rounded and lessened the chances of getting burned out. You learn so many different skills from playing different sports, too, so it's an extra advantage.

Tamika: My advice for young athletes is to work hard in everything they do. Sometimes we want things to come easy to us, but the things that come the easiest are sometimes things that aren't truly meant for us. Work hard!

Kenyon Catchings is a sales executive and the father of four sons.

Tamika Catchings is a four-time Olympic gold medalist and sixteen-year WNBA superstar with the Indiana Fever who currently serves as the director of player programs and franchise development with Pacers Sports & Entertainment.

Tauja Catchings is a former WNBA player and the executive director of the Catch the Stars Foundation.

MAKING IT BETTER

By James Lecesne

I never believed them. Ever.

When they told me that my love was a crime,

I thought they ought to be thrown in jail.

When they said that my love was a sin,

I politely wished them all to hell.

When I was informed that my love was considered a mental disease by the American Psychiatric Association and listed in the *Diagnostic and Statistical Manual of Mental Disorders* as a sociopathic personality disturbance, I rolled my eyes and called them crazy.

I was not a criminal.

I was not a sinner.

And I was definitely not crazy.

I was love.

Of course, back then I knew to keep quiet about my true identity. No one needed to know how different I was, how *other*. As young as five years old, I understood that I was not like my brother or my sisters or my parents, but there was no way I could have explained the situation to them. I grew up a gay boy in a New Jersey suburb at a time when it was still possible to never meet an openly gay person or hear the word *homosexual* spoken aloud. For most of my childhood, I assumed I was the only gay person in the world. So what could I have told my family? That I was a one-of-a-kind creation, a miracle, a unicorn? I had no words to describe my self to them back then. I only knew that I was love, plain and simple—but the kind that dared not speak its name.

By the time I was in middle school, however, it was obvious to me that love was going to be a problem. My schoolmates were beginning to couple up for make-out sessions; spin the bottle and "going steady" became things. I threw myself into these activities, hoping that I might be able to pass. But clearly my heart wasn't in it and everyone (especially the girls) could tell that I was faking. That's when the bullying began. The boys called me names; they used fists, sticks, and once a boot to make their point. And their point was very simple: I was unacceptable. This was the beginning of a very dark period for me. My teen years had barely begun and already I didn't see the point in going any further. Convinced that there was something fundamentally wrong with me, something that could not be fixed, I dimmed my wattage, became a brooding bystander, hid my love, and began to plan my escape.

What many people don't understand is that the struggle to be one's self as a young lesbian, gay, bisexual, transgender, or queer person is not primarily about the right to have sex how and with whom we want, or to pee where and when we please. These aspects are important, but it's really about our right to be fully and totally our selves—to be love—and then to be able to share that love with others. This seems as true today as it was for me back in the early 1970s, when no one was talking about the rights of LGBTQ people and the idea of gay youth did not exist. And though there is so much more acceptance nowadays for young people who are just discovering their identities, it's always been this urge to express and feel our love that fuels the movement and encourages us to find acceptance where we can.

In *Far from the Tree,* his groundbreaking book about parents, children, and the search for identity, Andrew Solomon writes about how some of us are born into families that don't share a trait that is essential to our selves. As a result, we must venture out beyond what he describes as our "vertical" families and find our "horizontal" families. "Vertical identities are usually respected as identities," writes Solomon. "Horizontal ones are often treated as flaws." And really, who wants to be identified by their flaws alone?

I was fifteen years old when I first ventured out to find my horizontal family. I was offered a job working as an apprentice at a summer-stock theater on the Jersey Shore. The opportunity was almost too good to be true: fourteen musicals in fourteen weeks, living in a room with ten other boys (including my best friend), working with actual actors, housing provided, meals as well. Maybe even the opportunity to perform in a few of the shows! But when my parents heard that I'd be working for free, they refused to let me go and instead insisted that I work another summer doing inventory at my father's Ford dealership.

For the first time in my young life, I realized that my life would simply not get better unless I myself did something to make it better. And so on the appointed day, while my parents were at work, I dared to climb into the back seat of a station wagon with my suitcase, in search of a new tribe. Eventually my parents must have realized that they'd lost this particular battle, and blessedly I've forgotten what surely must have followed—the fights on the phone, ultimatums, tears, threats, bargaining, and finally acquiescence to my plan.

It might sound overly dramatic to say that my experience at the Surflight Theatre shaped my future, but that summer certainly changed the course of my life. The choices I made regarding money, sex, integrity, friendship, work, style, success, and my fellow human beings were the first ones that I had to make on my own, and though many of those decisions were ill advised and impulsive and surely could've been avoided, they were, for better or worse, patently my own. It was then that I began to orient my life and livelihood toward the stage, recalibrating my expectations to include everything a life in the theater might offer. I came to understand for the first time the value of belonging to a community (both onstage and off). I found my tribe, my purpose, and I located a secret portal through which my self (small *s*) could be transported, enlarged, enriched, besparkled, and transformed into a bigger, better Self (big *S*)—not only for my own enjoyment, but also for the enjoyment of others. In other words, I found the love of my life.

And because I was working in the theater, I also had the opportunity to meet my first openly gay person. One day after rehearsal for the musical *Oliver!,* the director, who was not that much older than me, casually mentioned that he was a homosexual. And though the word was new to me, he patiently explained it to me: "It means I like boys."

"Cool," I replied. But for me it was way more than cool. The fact that there were boys (other than me) who unabashedly liked boys rocked my world and opened me up to the possibility that I could live a life that included love, the kind that was full-hearted and totally hot. Here was evidence that I could expand beyond my vertical family, and finally there was a name for what I was—and it wasn't *unicorn.*

Of course, the world has changed so much since I was a young adult in search of my lost tribe. These days the opportunities for young people to find people like themselves, to feel less isolated in their identities, and to openly express their love have grown exponentially. The increasing number of high school gay-straight alliances, the internet, and the growing acceptance within society of LGBTQ rights have made it much easier (and safer) for young people to expand their horizons and find the support they need to make the precarious journey from childhood to adulthood. And the Trevor Project, which I helped create almost twenty years ago, has been standing by ever since, providing suicide prevention and crisis intervention services for LGBTQ young people nation-wide.

The Trevor Project has also allowed me a place near the front lines as young adults struggle to realize their full potential. In the past few years, I've had the opportunity to meet some remarkable young people, many of whom are stepping up and making it better not only for themselves but for their peers as well. They've shown me what love can look like when we expand further beyond ourselves to make it better.

Jordan Scruggs was just thirteen when they realized that growing up gender nonconforming in rural Tennessee was going to be tough. One day in their own church, a fellow congregant verbally harassed them. Rather than walking away, Jordan began a campaign to transform their local church through dialogue. Not satisfied to make it better merely for themself, Jordan went on to personally visit LGBTQ-inclusive churches throughout Tennessee; they wanted to make sure they were not only gay friendly but gay affirming as well. A few years later, Jordan had created a directory of those safe places of worship for LGBTQ youth throughout their state.

At nineteen, Conner Mertens came out to his teammates, making him the first out college football player in the country. Not an easy thing for him to do, especially considering that he had three older brothers and a father who did not exactly welcome the idea. Fortunately, it turned out well for Conner, but he could imagine how badly it might have gone. And so he's founded Out on the Streets, an organization supporting young people who've been kicked out of their homes because of who they are.

When Jazz Jennings was just nine years old, she became an honorary cofounder, along with her parents, of TransKids Purple Rainbow Foundation, an organization that offers support to trans kids and their families. Not everyone is as lucky as Jazz is, to have parents who are so accepting and supportive, and this is something she's always known. So at twelve she started her own company, making and selling mermaid tails to raise money for the foundation. Now in high school, Jazz is still making it better for trans kids everywhere. She is a celebrated author, an activist, and the focus of a reality TV show.

These young people were raised with the belief that It Gets Better, but somehow they understood better than most that it doesn't get better without someone taking action. And they've taught me through their actions that making it better means making it big, making more and more my self, expanding self to include everything skin out. It's not enough to sit on the sidelines and hope that things will improve. If we want better, we will have to fight for it and then perhaps fight on behalf of others as well—all the others.

I've always believed that love is naturally generative. Love makes more: more opportunities, more family, more community, more and more connection. And whether it is romantic love, love for our fellow human beings, love for our Mother Earth, or love for ourselves, it is the secret ingredient that gets us to move beyond ourselves and into something bigger, better. I dream of the day LGBTQ youth throughout the world are afforded the same rights and opportunities as everyone else, and they are accepted for who and how they are. Can we be that big? Of course we can. We are love.

 James Lecesne is a cofounder of the Trevor Project, the only nationwide twenty-four-hour suicide prevention and crisis intervention lifeline for LGBTQ youth.

THEY DIDN'T SUCCEED—
I SURVIVED

By Fanny Starr

My name is Fanny Starr; I am ninety-six years old, I am a Holocaust survivor, and I speak for the Six Million who cannot speak for themselves.

I don't know the year or the month that the Lodz Ghetto was liquidated, but a history book tells me it was August 1944. As it was happening, my whole family, and others, walked to the train tracks. It was late in the afternoon, and it was the last time I saw my home in Lodz, Poland.

As the ghetto was liquidating, the Nazi commander told us that our new residence, Paradise, would offer us hot showers, doctors, and clean living conditions. I clung to my parents and my siblings, not knowing it would be the last time we held each other.

My whole family was loaded into one cattle car, roughly sixty family members along with other people. All of us were packed in tight with no room to move. We had no bathroom, and the train smelled like human waste. Soon we would all smell like human waste.

For days the train just went back and forth, never stopping. We could tell we were covering the same path over and over, which only worsened the experience by disorienting us. We stood on our feet the whole time, and our legs became sore from standing so long. We had no food or water. Children cried, and adults cried. We were treated like animals, animals being carted off to the slaughterhouses.

Finally the train arrived at Auschwitz. The train stopped so sharply that we all jerked into each other, and the most tired among us fell and could not stand back up.

We walked down the planks, clinging to one another for life. None of us knew what was about to happen to us. The SS officers greeted us, and helping the SS officers were young Jewish male prisoners—the *Sonderkommandos*—forced to labor and assist in the demise of their own people.

The whole family was in one line. We held each other as we received directions from Dr. Josef Mengele, later known as the Angel of Death. He told us, *"Arbeit macht das Leben süß,"*—work makes life sweet—and he pointed to the sign over the gates at the entrance into Auschwitz. *Arbeit macht frei*—work makes you free.

While Dr. Mengele was speaking, my father disappeared into the crowds, sensing something was wrong. The SS officers began dividing us up under the watchful eye of Dr. Mengele. Dr. Mengele made the selection with his thumb: those whom he pointed to the right would live, and those who went to the left would die. His gesture became known as *who shall live and who shall die.*

The SS officers offered a shower after the long journey to those who were directed to the left. The first in line were the elderly, the disabled, and little children along with their mothers. My cousins, my baby brother, and my mommy were selected to go to take a shower. We soon learned the "showers" were filled with Zyklon B nerve gas. That was the last time I saw my baby brother and my mommy. I yelled to Mommy, "Mommy, I love you." Mommy was crying and screaming as she walked away in fear toward the unknown.

My daddy and my other brother were transported to Dachau concentration camp. It would be decades before I knew whether they survived. I was finally reunited with my brother in 1964, and he told me that our daddy had died in his lap, that he'd given up living and starved himself to death.

Back in Auschwitz, we could not cry because the tears would get us killed immediately. I clung to my sister Rena; she's younger than me by six years. We stood in a line and gave our names, our dates of birth, and the cities in which we were born. I did not get a tattoo, nor did my sister or anyone else on our transport, though to this day I do not know why.

My sister and I marched into a large warehouse; we took off all our clothes and left them there. The SS shaved my head and handed me a striped dress with a number sewn on it. I did not get a pair of underwear or a bra, just a pair of wooden clogs. I had no name to the Nazis; I was now a number.

All of us women looked similar, bald and wearing striped dresses; I started shouting for my sister Rena, pleading, "Where are you?"

I heard my name, "Fela," and I walked toward the voice calling out to me. My sister and I clutched one another, and I never let go from that moment on.

I had to go to the bathroom, so the SS women took many of

us, including my sister, along with two German shepherd dogs. When we came to the bathroom, I saw my aunts, my daddy's sisters. But they, too, were being taken away. That was the last time I saw them.

The SS shouted commands at us, and I was reminded over and over, *"Arbeit macht frei."* We were put into rows of three women across; all in all, roughly six hundred to one thousand women marched to an open field.

The SS women shouted at us, *"Sich hinsetzen"*—sit down. I looked up at the sky and saw it was red like blood, and it smelled like burning flesh. This ashen white snow was falling everywhere. Suddenly I realized it wasn't snow; it was ashes from the chimney falling on my sister and me. I cried silently, knowing those ashes were the remains of my baby brother and mommy. That's when I lost my faith in G-d.

We sat in silence, looking at the SS women. The days became nights and the nights became days, no food, no water, just starvation as we sat in the field. I don't know for how many days or weeks we sat in that field.

Eventually the last transport train arrived from the Lodz Ghetto to Auschwitz. The SS women had us stand up to march. We marched toward the crematorium and saw a man being carried on a large chair. The man was Mordechai Rumkowski.

Rumkowski was the head of the Lodz Ghetto, like a mayor. He had promised to protect the children of Lodz and had given a speech to people of the ghetto years earlier, which later became known as "Give Me Your Children." But we soon learned that he was a mass murderer who helped the Nazis, hoping they would keep him safe in return.

Right after that speech, my father heard the hospital was

going to be raided. We ran to get my mommy, who was sick with pleurisy. As we arrived at the hospital, we saw the soldiers arriving, too. They immediately went to the maternity ward.

They were not there to protect the children, as Rumkowski had promised. We watched as the soldiers took the newborn babies, laughing as they ripped them into pieces. The soldiers started going room to room, looking for women in labor, and tore their babies out of their stomachs. They took those innocent babies and smashed them against the wall and then shot the mothers. To this day, I ask G-d, *Why?*

I bore witness with my sister, and all the other women, as Mordechai Rumkowski, who helped the Nazis so he could help himself, was carried on a chair to the ovens. The SS officers and the commander of Auschwitz, Rudolf Höss, laughed with glee as they burned Rumkowski alive.

While in Auschwitz, I encountered another legendary evil figure of the Nazi regime. Irma Grese, nicknamed the Beautiful Beast, was one of Hitler's elite SS women. I first witnessed Grese's wickedness as she was guarding us in the field at Auschwitz.

One day she walked around us women sitting in the field with her riding crop. Something happened that upset her, and she called out to two women. They got up and walked to her. Grese started shouting at them in German; she took the riding crop and wrapped it around one woman's neck. She strangled the woman to death for no apparent reason, right before my eyes, then did the same thing to the other woman.

Eventually the day came when we were transported to another concentration camp, called Ravensbrück. Ravensbrück was a camp just for women. The SS women shouted at my sister, the others, and me as we were loaded into an open coal car, in the cold, to remember, *"Arbeit macht frei."*

The Holocaust is long over, but its evil and its effects still linger today. How did we allow such heinous crimes against humanity to be committed, and why does the world continue to kill innocent people?

I will never forget and I will never forgive the murderers, and every day I cry. I cry because I miss my daddy, my mommy, my older sister, and my baby brother. A total of five of us survived from my family, out of sixty: my sister Rena, my brother Cuba, my cousin Helen, my uncle Max, and myself.

To this day, I do not know how I survived. I have a mission to tell the world about evil after being victimized over and over. G-d knows I'm gentle, and I do well by helping others in sharing my strength. We feed the homeless every week, because I know what it is like to starve. I want people to care for each other and to be kind to one another. Though individual acts of kindness may seem small, even forgettable in the moment, they can mean survival to someone.

We cannot change history, but we can work to prevent it from repeating itself. Every day we see old wounds resurfacing. We are seeing the rise of nationalist ideologies here in my beloved America, the same ideologies I saw in Poland as a child. I speak to young people because they are my hope. I tell my story to let others who have suffered, who still suffer, know that they are not alone. I fight for righteousness so it will never happen again.

The internet has empowered the Nazi movements and the Holocaust deniers, and yet it has also made it possible for many to explore the Holocaust and learn more about the horrors that I and so many others witnessed and for me to share my story. We all leave our footprints on society, and in the age of social media, we leave a long trail in the digital world. Together, our voices and our stories can lift each other up and let those who wish to do harm to us, and to humanity, know that we will resist.

 Fanny Starr is a ninety-six-year-old Holocaust survivor.

LEARNING ABOUT EMPATHY

By Imran Siddiquee

On that morning in September, like most mornings in high school, I walked into class already on edge. It was first period, a foreign language class, and I sat nervously next to my friend Mark. I liked talking to Mark, but I still worried that he might ask me about a game I hadn't watched, or that Jill, who sat nearby, might notice me noticing her—not to mention the fear I had that Mrs. R. might give us a pop quiz on some vocabulary I hadn't studied.

It was the beginning of twelfth grade, and by then I had learned to keep my head down, as a brown-skinned boy in the Midwest. When I was younger, after the Oklahoma City bombing in 1995, our mosque had been burned to the ground by neo-Nazis. So I understood, or at least I thought I did, the danger that existed, and the path I had to take to be a "good" Muslim in the United States. Yet when self-doubt struck—as it often did—my go-to tools as a young man weren't that unique: silence, suppression, and a simmering kind of resentment.

But regardless of what was going well, the minute I was inside the doors of the school—passing by all the more attractive, more athletic white boys—I would feel the claustrophobia of unattainable expectation creep up. I would remember the reality of American high school, and of what I looked like, the fog of masculinity and culture and religion I was always swimming through. So I'd look down and away, or—more often than not—I would join the guys making awkward jokes about girls and sex, to avoid thinking about how strange it was to have this feeling of inevitable failure inside. And even though outside those walls my best friends were girls, I'd sit only with boys at lunch. Sometimes we'd dare each other to do something ridiculous at the table and actually call it "man club."

On this day, though, everything was heightened—because I knew that something else was going on in the world. I don't recall if I had heard it on the radio while driving to school, or if I had seen a report on TV before leaving home, but I do remember being the one to tell Mrs. R. that we might want to turn on CNN. That there had been an incident in New York.

The sound of the news report soon became the only sound in the room. Was that debris or people falling from the windows? Did someone say it was probably Muslims who did this? Were people looking at me?

Most of what happened next blurs together, but at some point—after they showed more frightening images of the scene in Manhattan on-screen and the commentators repeatedly said the word *terrorism*—Mrs. R. asked me what I thought was going on. She posed this question out loud, for everyone to hear.

A part of me assumed that this was related to the fact that I was the one who had told her to turn the TV on in the first place. Or that I was chatting loudly with Mark about the failures of George W. Bush. Maybe she'd overheard? Surely there were teenagers in classrooms all around the country answering the same question from their teachers right then—because they were articulate and well informed.

But other parts of me know, and knew then, that it was something else. That I was the only one with a beard and brown skin, the only one with a name like mine. What frustrates me most is how I responded nevertheless, how much I wanted to believe that my intelligence—my niceness—could protect me. How I reached for appeasement.

Though I had been bullied since grade school, the truth is, I knew there was a path to (superficial) acceptance in this community. Like most boys, I knew that bullying others was available to me, but within that, so was whiteness. Or at least proximity to it. I could align myself with the straight white boys, put others and myself down, and I could not only be seen as cool, but also be given my own kind of tangential power. Safety within an exaggerated masculinity.

Maybe that's why I said that the people on TV might be right. Why I mentioned, in front of everybody, that we didn't know if it was terrorists from Muslim countries, but that there were reasons to believe that this could be the case. My first instinct was to both admit complicity and stress my innocence, as if I were on trial and the most important thing was to be a reliable narrator. My family was from Bangladesh, after all, not one of those "extremist" countries. I added that I had relatives who lived in New York, too. I assured all the white people that I felt what they felt.

After first period, after the horror had settled in a bit, we returned to the hallways. We were teenagers again—still. But everything was changing, or at least it felt that way to me. As I stood at my locker with my backpack, the smell of home-cooked meals clinging to that space, I felt pushed to the edge. I kept my head down and did my best to hide all that was bubbling up.

But I felt weak, and weakness felt like a mistake. I needed to do something to regain control.

So I marched into the principal's office, pretending I had all the answers—trying to will this fantasy of manliness into existence. In that stale room, where I had to wait behind a brown desk for what felt like an eternity, I raised my voice and demanded that something be done. I told the principal that this was our Pearl Harbor and that we should send everyone home. (In truth, I didn't know much about Pearl Harbor. I just wanted to talk to my family. To be with my mom.) He said no. Everything was fine. I was sent back to class.

The next period was a social studies class, which I thought might be a safer place. The teacher seemed to like me, and he had studied American government and history, so surely he would understand the broader context. Maybe he could explain the attack to me. But instead, like the other white teachers that day, he just briefly looked at me with sympathy before asking if I wanted to come up and talk. If I could explain.

Standing at the front of another distraught class, trying to find the words for why people who looked like me apparently wanted to kill everyone, I could think about only the pimples on my nose. The way I was sweating, and how even though I ironed my clothes each morning, by this point in the day they always seemed wrinkled again. How strange my face must have looked while I tried to hold back the tears.

In the weeks after September 11, things remained surreal. There were all the conversations about Islam at school—with peers and teachers—and the 24-7 cycle of fear on TV. People calling me Osama in the hallways. The not-so-random way I was pulled out of a security line at the airport. I started to detach from my family and friends, even as I continued to play my part on the surface. I smiled for the cameras when we were profiled by the local paper (look at these nice Muslims!). I took my AP exams and got into college. Yet there was this nagging feeling that I was to blame for all the pain around me, made worse by a sense of martyrdom. Real men don't cry, and if they don't turn to violence, they turn to other forms of control—over others and over themselves. I became depressed, and a year later, when I was a freshman at the University of Illinois, that depression led to self-harm.

Yet many of the questions I have now are not for my teenage self, but for the people in power around me—especially the men. Like most adolescent boys, I still looked to men for guidance, for some model of how to handle my emotions "like a man." On that terrifying day, why didn't any of them ask me how I was doing? Afterward, why didn't anyone try to make me feel safe? While the world was demonizing those who looked like me, I wandered my school hiding from windows and mirrors. Afraid to see in my own reflection the danger and weakness that I heard others whispering about. Afraid of the truth I could feel—that I would never be "man enough" to feel safe in this country. All while most of the adult men in my life were dealing with the situation in much the same way: exuding toughness, avoiding emotion.

To move on from that moment required me to find new tools, new mentors. I had to step outside myself and my own experience as a boy and admit that I was lost. I had to unlearn my idealization of whiteness and manhood. But I hadn't really been taught how to do this, or where to turn, or that it was even possible to turn to people beyond the men who led my school, my mosque, and my country.

Looking back, I can see now that I made it through that period only by following the people who weren't caught up in the tangle of performing masculinity. The community members who came together in love, not fear or entitlement. The family and friends who opened their arms without ever asking me to "man up," and who listened to me even as I questioned my faith. Muslim women who made space for me, even when I didn't always make the same space for them. The feminists of color who gave me a deeper understanding of the society I live in. In fact, the most empathetic folks in my life back then were those who were left more vulnerable than I was in this new landscape—and I eventually realized that this was no coincidence.

Many years later, on the day when the courts let George Zimmerman free after he murdered an unarmed Black teenager named Trayvon Martin, I was pulled back to high school, to what I said to my French class that morning. I wandered onto the streets of the Mission District in San Francisco, feeling despair and anger as helicopters circled above the protests forming in the distance. I felt a connection then not because my youth was comparable to Martin's, but precisely because it was so different. How I had had the choice to be protected by pseudowhiteness as a kid, and the ongoing privilege of a middle-class life in America. How lucky I was that some women decided to show me love in a world that so often showed them hate.

Understanding the intersections of white supremacy and patriarchy—the way ideologies of dominance are part of the very structure of this country—and how they condition men for violence, regardless of their station in life, was a part of this journey. I found I had similarities with the straight white men who had hurt me, as well as differences from those with whom I had been lumped together as a Muslim American man. I had to revisit all those jokes I made in high school, all the times I dismissed the voices of women. I left my religion after I grew disillusioned with masculinity overall, but more importantly, in this process I found a new purpose.

I was taught empathy, not the presumptuous kind—the kind that says, for instance, that I could ever truly understand what it's like to be a Black trans woman in a country that hates women, trans people, and Black people—but rather the kind of empathy that reminds you, and allows you to stand in awe of, how much you will never know about the lives of those more marginalized than you. Persistence, for me, has been about letting go of the need for absolute knowledge, for control—moving myself from the center as much as possible—and supporting those who are most passionately resisting the status quo. Accepting that I will mess up, but always working toward being more sensitive, expressive, and compassionate. Speaking up against bullying, misogyny, and the violence of men in power.

Following the lead of women of color, including Muslim women, and resisting the pull of hypermasculinity as much as I can hasn't just made me feel personally safer in the United States, it's made me realize my own ability, and responsibility, to make the world safer for others—including that younger version of me.

This has been an unquantifiable gift, and a guiding light in my life since.

 Imran Siddiquee is a writer, a filmmaker, and an activist working to transform how gender and race are represented in the media.

THE ROOTS
OF EMBODIED EDUCATION

By Liz Wolfson

I was born the fourth child in a family of competitive athletes, with three older brothers. They are eight, six, and two and a half years older than me. The story of my birth is legendary—my father was the first father allowed in the delivery room of the small-town hospital where I was born, and when I descended from my mother's womb, the doctor announced, "It's a girl!" and everyone cheered. The doctor lifted me in the air and spread my legs for my father so that he could see I had a vagina. My mother said, "Sanford, that's the end of your family," and he said, "This is no place to discuss this," and she said, "This is the last time we will ever discuss it!" And thus began my life.

My birth announcement is a black-and-white picture of my three older brothers, all with crew-cut hair, the littlest holding a basketball. They are all smiling. The tagline reads: "Thank Heaven for Little Girls."

We were all reared on a backyard basketball court, where we learned how to use both hands for layups and I was trained never to let my brothers knock me down. When I was in middle school, our small town formed its first all-girls middle school basketball team; within one season we became the top-ranked middle school team in the state, based on our record of playing other country-bumpkin teams in the area. But as we ventured out to play the more experienced urban teams, we learned we weren't that great, getting our asses kicked in the first round of the state tournament by some South Jersey city slickers. But we worked hard, and by the time I captained our high school team, we were legitimate state contenders and made it as far as the sectional finals, losing only two games away from becoming the state champions.

What I knew then was that being a girl or being feminine meant being soft, pretty, and chased after by the boys. That car doors were to be opened for me when a boy was around. That the prettiest girls were cheerleaders, and that getting dressed up meant dresses for me and suits for my brothers, and that boys were rough-and-tumble while girls were tickled for kicks and baked cookies and cakes.

Daily life went something like this: I set the table and cleared the table—all three courses—every night, and my brothers took out the trash. I took care of the plants and flowers indoors, and they did yard work. I had a curfew, and they publicly talked about their escapades with girls (and even, once, a girl's mother). My brothers were allowed to question my friend choices, my boyfriend choices, and I was to abide by their opinions. I was relegated to smiling prettily and letting boys look at me as their opinions were thrust upon me. I was told not to go out on Sunday, because bad things happen to little girls who go out on Sunday. My brothers commented on my mother's looks and my looks all the time. Only I had to visit my infirm grandmother every night while home from college, because this is what mothers and daughters do.

I suppose that much of this reality was a function of the times, but that didn't help me when I got my period and needed to buy tampons and nobody wanted to talk about it. It didn't help me when I saw my brothers chasing a babysitter and one of them felt her up and nobody wanted to talk about it. When I was graduating from eighth grade and my brother's college friend was "interested" in me and everyone thought that was cute and funny and nobody wanted to talk about it.

I recall being about ten years old and watching a high school basketball game from the wrestling room, a closed-in loft space one floor up, at the far end of the court. I would often retreat there during games and do cartwheels and other gymnastics as an older brother starred below. There was a viewing window through which I would stick my head and watch intermittently as the crowd roared. Once, before I went up, I remember my father watching the varsity cheerleaders and talking to someone, saying, "Now, that is a pretty girl."

I remember the sensation in the curious pit of my stomach as I climbed the stairs and then looked out the window while the girls in their short skirts and sweaters and matching saddle shoes ran onto center court, hands steady on their hips. And there *she* was, the bustiest and perkiest of young women, clapping her hands, waving her arms, and stomping her feet in support of the male athletes.

I was neither of those things, nor would I grow into either of those things, and therefore I was never to be the pretty girl. So as I tumbled around in the wrestling room that day, it became clear to my young mind and heart that I had a choice to make—to become that cheerleader, or to become my brother starring on the court and being cheered for. I made the clear-cut decision to be my brother on the court.

From my freshman year in high school, I was an accomplished athlete in three sports and surpassed all three of my brothers in all-around accolades, including a Division I athletic experience.

I remember being a senior in high school and the top eleven field hockey players in the state had just been announced on the front page of the Sunday newspaper. The name of each girl was listed, along with her high school, position, height, and weight, followed by a glorious caricature and a paragraph explaining her strengths of play and why she was chosen. I made the team.

One of the most memorable experiences of that celebratory time was the shame I felt at being listed as weighing 135 pounds. Only one other person on the roster was within fifteen pounds of me. I was a fast and nimble midfielder, so there was a disconnect. And I remember two of my family members spending an entire car ride to school the next day discussing how they had had no idea I weighed so much. I remember wanting to disappear.

I spent so much of my childhood discombobulated by gender roles and gender stereotypes.

As a girl, I was a secret weapon on the court. My mother sat on the sidelines and often knit. I would sail shots through the hoop, and if an opposing (male) player tried to bump me, my older brothers would feign bravado and we would all laugh. When I reached the one-thousand-point milestone in high school, my middle brother—who had been the last player in our high school to do this, six years before—could not have been prouder. Yet in college, when my first real boyfriend challenged me to a game of one-on-one—and there was no way his skills rivaled mine—I asked for guidance, as I knew instinctively that beating a guy wasn't my road to successfully landing a husband. The guidance I had always received was to "let men be men."

In my lifetime, sports has been a primary and consistent venue for strong, powerful, and high-achieving women to experience the lessons of prowess, risk, resiliency, and power from a young age. So as I began to develop my own expression of my personal femininity that emanated from the court and field, I discovered that deferring to boys and men on and off the court was not a path of expression by any means, but an act of compliance. And I am not a compliant being. So I did play my boyfriend one-on-one, and I won the game easily. And I knew then that I was beautiful.

I know that my story is not wholly unique. I also know that my story can serve as motivation for other young girls to find their voices through organized sports, including rigorous movement like dance and performance. I tell my story so that others can burst out of their gender-stereotyped realities and not feel alone, because I insist on living in a world where the cacophony of voices of young women is loud and strong, where it emanates from the court or from the field or from wherever necessary. Living in my world of movement as a young woman was freedom.

It is my belief that we can build whole schools that teach this freedom of movement as an organic part of growing up. As girls and women, we should seek out fully embodied experiences whenever possible. They keep us free.

I will do everything in my power to help. Thank Heaven for little girls.

 Liz Wolfson is the chief visionary officer of Girls Athletic Leadership Schools.

NOT A DOLL

By Jadaida Glover

A lady is supposed to be this prim, proper, Holy Ghost–filled woman. She is supposed to speak only when spoken to, stay perfect and sweet and still like the delicate flower she is. I am loud and silly and tomboyish. I wear pants rather than skirts and dresses. I speak my mind rather than remain mute. And so I am deemed wild and unladylike.

At church, the women whisper about me. "She ain't got no morals," they say, and "What kind of virtuous woman can be acting like that?" These women are from every inch of the Bible Belt. They are from places where women aren't to speak to men or they'll be branded "fast." So when they see me bike riding or playing catch with the guys, me all smiles and "no modesty," laughing with these young men, I become the talk of the church.

At school, a girl is supposed to wear full-face makeup and be afraid of sports. She will never get a boyfriend if she is a tomboy. She is supposed to be a beauty queen—flawless makeup, hair down her back, and dressed to kill. But I continue to walk around with my hair twisted or braided, maybe pinned in a bun; my makeup basic, eyeliner, lipstick, and eye shadow; and my wardrobe based on however I feel that day.

And so I keep to myself. I don't bother anyone. I sit in the library, doing my homework, and still this girl comes and sits down next to me. I recognize her from one of my classes, and although we have never actually said a word to each other, I always thought she seemed harmless. But now she's bursting with something she's just waiting to spill. I sit there, pretending to be reading my book, but I'm actually watching her. I watch as she leans on the table, her bottom lip crushed under her teeth and her right leg shaking with anticipation. Finally I can't take it anymore. I put my book down, purse my lips, and fold my hands. As if on cue, she leans in closer and with the widest grin asks me, "Is it true?"

I give her the most confused look I can muster and smirk. "Is what true, beloved?"

The grin on her face widens. "That you're, you know . . . a lesbian?"

And just like that, I realize I am the talk of the school.

At every family event, I'm bombarded with, "Why can't you act ladylike?" They want me to be a demure young woman who is obsessed with makeup. They want me to love fashion and always wear skirts and dresses (not going to happen). They want me to be the perfect lady at church, and the perfect girlfriend at school.

Sometimes it feels like I'm trapped. At church, school, and home, they tell me who I should be, and their voices are so loud it's hard to find myself. I want to please everyone, but when I do as they wish, they critique every detail of what I've done. One Sunday, even though I swore I'd wear only pants, I decide to wear a black dress with blue sandals and do some light makeup. I think

I look really cute. I even post pictures on Facebook. My aunt is appalled and the rest of the church snickers. The comments on the pictures are horrible. Isn't this what they want? Isn't this what they have been waiting for? But they say the colors are off and the eye shadow doesn't suit me, and suddenly I feel so incredibly small. I left home so confident, only to be picked apart when I'm doing the very thing they ask me to. It's confusing and frustrating, and it leaves me feeling emptier than ever.

I am empty when an older deacon approaches me at church. He wears a lopsided grin as he sits down beside me and tells me he wants to talk about the testimony I am scheduled to give at the service. He does not think I should speak. As he talks, I tilt my head to the left, keeping my face devoid of emotion, completely calm. He says a girl such as myself should not consider setting foot on a podium when she hasn't even mastered the art of being a virtuous woman. He points to my beige linen pants and says that no true lady would dress as masculinely as I do. I chuckle a little, and the emptiness rumbles in my belly, but I let him continue. He advises that I be trained by the women of the church and probably wait until next year to speak.

Now I'm not chuckling, I'm smiling. I hold up my left hand and tell him what I have learned in church about being a virtuous woman. She is a woman who knows her worth and will not compromise her standards to fit those of the world around her. She is hardworking, and she delights herself in the Lord. The deacon eagerly agrees, happy that I have proved his point, expecting me to bow out of next week's service. But instead I put my hands in my lap and tell him that I have just described myself.

I'm not empty anymore. I fill myself with truth. A lady is anything she wants to be. She can be loud and silly and tomboyish.

She can speak her mind and stand strong. A lady is an unmovable, unshakable force to be reckoned with.

Now when my family asks me why I can't act ladylike, I slide to the front of my seat, lean my elbows on my knees, and say, "Who wrote this book on what is and isn't ladylike?" I ask them why it matters that I prefer pants to dresses. I question why speaking my mind bothers them.

And then I speak my mind, and I speak it loud. I am not some doll that they can turn into whomever they want. I am tired of these stereotypes that are attached to our gender. Women aren't created to be trophies to be gawked at. We aren't created to sit still and look pretty.

Every day I break down the stereotype of who I should be as a woman.

 Jadaida Glover is a graduate of the High School for Medical Professions in Brooklyn, New York, and was a mentee at Girls Write Now.

THE QUIETLY RELENTLESS

By Soraya Chemaly

As a child, more than practically anything else, I loved reading. Almost always, I had a book with me. Rain or shine. In cars, at church, riding to and from school. One of my favorite things to do was finish one Nancy Drew mystery per day, something a friend and I raced to do first. By the time I was eleven or twelve, my interest in reading had become an interest in researching and writing. All three activities were, together, a game. Books were mysteries. History was a puzzle. Trying to understand how I came to be where I was became my favorite pastime. I lived in a place, however, where reading wasn't of interest to many people. It wasn't important, particularly if you were a girl, and especially a teenage girl. Even when I was given books, they were overwhelmingly shaped by stereotypes. For several years in a row, for example, I was given the exact same book about a ballerina. It was not one but two shades of pink. Flower arranging was also high on other people's lists of things I should read about. There is nothing inherently wrong with either topic—it was just that I wasn't particularly interested in ballet or flowers. I was interested in history and science. When summer came along each year, I wanted nothing more than to spend my days immersed in books and dusty records. I lived in the Bahamas, and in the summer, most of my classmates and friends were lazing around their houses trying to keep cool, taking care of siblings, going to the beach, or working. I wanted to do none of those things. I wanted to read and write. To be sure, being able to do this was a luxury. I did not have to contribute financially to my family's well-being or pay for my own food or schooling. But it was also a very specific challenge in a place where valuing the life of the mind—not only as a privilege, but as a necessity, as a way of changing your life—seemed to be neither a priority nor a virtue. Wanting to spend sunny summer days studying may not seem odd or countercultural in some places or in some families, but in others, this simple interest or desire represents multiple levels of confrontation.

My mother, in her quietly subversive way, thought that what I wanted to do was a good idea. She ignored curious comments or social disparagement, and for several years, with my younger siblings in tow, she drove me to the National Archives. Every morning she dropped me off, and every evening she came back, hours later, to pick me up. This was support enough, but while there I met another woman. Dr. Gail Saunders was a historian and the head archivist. I didn't know her when I first appeared in the space she was responsible for building. Every day I would show up and go through the process of scrolling through index files and making requests from back rooms and high shelves. She didn't have to take me seriously, but she did. She patiently and with formality brought papers, books, and records to the desk where I sat in an overchilled room, which, in my memory, had no windows. The books, kept since the late seventeenth century by the British government and church, were massive and leather-bound. Some stretched two to three feet when opened flat. They were covered in beautiful, often fading, black ink script. I remember her wearing gloves. She showed me how to handle paper that was hundreds of years old without damaging it. She talked to me about how the lettering worked and differed from our own. She taught me to operate a microfilm machine, how to load it and scroll through images. Soon she brought me books without my having to ask and would talk to me about them. She was patient and kind, and her patience and kindness encouraged me to keep searching. It's hard to express how exceptional her attention was and how important it was to know that there was a person who took my ideas seriously.

There were many days when someone would admonish me for disappearing into this building instead of doing what most of the other kids I knew were doing. I could be helping my mother at home or my father at work. I could be socializing with friends. There was always the suggestion that what I was doing was odd and, ultimately, selfish. There were also other days when what I was doing seemed silly or fruitless, even to me. What did it matter what people had done two or three hundred years ago? Who cared whether or not we had Puritans or pirates, slaves or slave owners, in our past? No one seemed that interested. But each summer morning, for weeks on end and for several years, I walked into the cool and quiet building and read, wrote, and talked to someone who cared deeply about history and had worked hard to be able to do so.

I first met Dr. Saunders in the summer of 1979. In 2015, I

called her to thank her. She had no memory of me, my questions, or my comings and goings, but she was happy to hear from me nonetheless.

When we spoke, three things struck me. The first was that she, a woman of mixed race in a country that was a colony in the throes of fighting for independence, had overcome tremendous obstacles to achieve what she had achieved. The second was that she selflessly, openly, and eagerly shared her knowledge and experience with me, a child she didn't know at all. She influenced me and the course of my life tremendously, and her willingness to take the time to teach me how to think about history made my insistence and persistence possible. Third, in both her case and mine, it was clear that pursuing our intellectual interests meant challenging stereotypes and the tidal force of culture. We were constantly confronting gender expectations and socially prescribed constraints related to ethnicity and race. A woman and a girl dedicated to thinking about history were easily considered transgressive. Our pursuits were defined by our own interests, not those of others. Our time was spent nurturing ideas, not other people. We prioritized ourselves, a problem for women still today. Thirty-five years after meeting, we talked about all this, often laughing during our hour-long long-distance conversation.

I realized that she was much younger in 1979 than I as we spoke. Thirty-five years after we first met, we talked openly as adults about gender, race, and the colonialism that we were born into. We discussed how our families, our spouses, and our choice of work affected us. We continued to share mutual curiosities and an endless fascination with the relationship of the past, present, and future. I was very happy to have found her and had the chance to thank her, so many years later. I will always be grateful for the many hours that she spent cultivating my curiosity, determination, and, yes, persistence.

 Soraya Chemaly is a writer and activist whose work focuses on the role of gender in culture, politics, religion, and media.

MORE THAN MY WOMB

By Melissa Marr

I grew up rural. That's a euphemism for *poor*, incidentally. My parents wouldn't use the word. We had indoor plumbing, we had land to grow vegetables, and we bathed regularly. My mother says, "We had a good home." My father points out, "We never went hungry." As an adult, I realize definitions are subjective, but the truth of it is that I didn't know I was poor.

My mother's mother used to come around with a lawn bag full of clothes. Put in what you outgrew; take out what fit. New old clothes. On birthdays, clothes and books were the dream gifts. Summer was better. I wore my bikini while I worked in the garden and hung the laundry on the line, and when it got too hot, I cooled off in the pool. Poor people don't have pools. Clearly, we weren't poor. The neighbors up the hill had to swim in water with crawfish and snakes.

It's all relative.

My mother had grown up in an area in the Appalachians called Pole Creek Hollow. You pronounce that middle word *crick*, by the way—unless you're uppity. By the time I was a teen, I was uppity by choice. I surrendered *crick* and *hain't* and added some *g*'s to the ends of words that used to end with *-in'*. I spoke slowly and learned to pronounce the bigger words in books. When I'm angry, my *g*'s all fall away, and my cussin' gets worse. I don't spit, though. I don't brawl. I don't . . . a lot of things that come quite naturally to me, even after a couple of academic degrees, two professional careers, and traveling around the world.

It's still all relative, though: how I define myself, how they define me, and what any of it means. We all agree that I'm uppity, but we aren't meaning the word the same.

My parents think I'm ashamed of where I come from. I'm not. Where I come from made me who I am. I came out of a town where being a girl meant I ought to be married and having babies before I was old enough to drink legally. It meant that "college" was an associate's degree at one of the community colleges so as to get a better job. It meant that you "made do" and didn't air your dirty laundry.

I think about that last bit a lot as I write, as I dodge interview questions, as I decide if I'll let anyone read this. It's not that I'm ashamed. If anything, I'm proud, but if people looked at that place, those people, *my* people, they'd look at them with curiosity or disdain or maybe that strange, precious thing where country folk are somehow wiser and truer. They're not. They're people. They love, and they hate. They have prejudices.

It doesn't mean there aren't obstacles that come from being born a girl in such a world.

By the time I was fifteen, two of my friends had babies. By seventeen, there were six babies altogether from my friends my age. It wasn't shocking. It wasn't even always a cause for alarm. Two of the mothers were married. Girls had babies. Preened and wore too much makeup. Sassed and shimmied into jeans too tight and heels too high.

What it meant to be a girl was to make babies, to advertise the goods so as to fill the womb, and to keep a man.

My mother succeeded. My parents were married when my mother was seventeen, young but not as young as *her* mother. Gin (my mother's mother) had married at fourteen. By the time Gin was seventeen, she'd had a few babies. Two of them lived. In comparison to her mother, *my* mother was not too young to marry.

There were a lot of things that were defined by comparison.

My aunts were married with babies before seventeen. My mother has the honor of being the only one of the six living siblings to not only have graduated from high school but to have done it under her maiden name. Of course, she married my father the following Saturday and moved into a mobile home that he had purchased "off the mountain."

A woman's worth was tied to making babies and keeping a good home. Any manner of dress, attitude, or misstep could be forgiven if a woman caught a "good" man who had a "good" job and they made a "good" home. My mother, her mother, her sisters, their daughters, my neighbors—they were all succeeding.

Sometimes relative definition sucks.

At fifteen, I was told I couldn't make babies. A rape—which my mother explained as "just what happens to girls"—had damaged me internally. I was useless as a woman. What kind of good man wants a woman who can't give him babies? It was bad enough that I was bookish, used big words, and wanted to go to college. Now I was broken, too.

There were things in my life that knocked me down. The rape was one. PTSD as a result of the rape was another. A man who said he loved me but laid hands on me . . . a couple of men like him, if I am truly honest. A go-round with anorexia because I thought that being prettier might overcome being broken. All of them came down to one truth: figuring out what it means to be a woman.

Where we are rooted feeds us. Some of that food is toxic. Being a girl should *not* mean being raped. It should *not* mean being advised to return to the arms of the man who bloodied me. It should *not* mean hiding a drive to learn, or sacrificing it because it makes me uppity.

I am more than my womb. It took a long time to realize that. It wasn't my degrees, or the countries I visited, or the contracts I signed. It was the slow, steady realization that I have worth for the work I do and the people whose lives I touch. Being a woman doesn't mean I can't be a useful part of society through my work. Being a woman doesn't mean that I am here only to mind kids and catch a man. I saw it in the results of my teaching and now I see it in the reactions of my readers. I see it when I teach workshops, sign books, donate my time and money. I see it when I offer a ride to my neighbor or give my time in pursuit of my faith. I am of worth because I strive to make G-d's world, *our* world, a better place.

I am more than my roots, but they are a part of me. I worked my way through college and graduate school. I bake from scratch, as my mother and her mother did. I do not reject the beautiful parts of my heritage, but I do not accept the limits imposed upon me because I was born with a womb. It is a part of me, but not all of me.

I embrace my accent a bit more these days. I let it slip even in business meetings or silly posh events. I wear lovely dresses mostly bought at thrift stores, because success doesn't erase frugality, and my many tattoos show. I practice historical sword fighting. It makes me feel strong and powerful. I negotiate contracts. It makes me remember that I am allowed to want. I create stories, tells truths, air the sullied linens, take risks, and do not bow my head. I will not be broken or ashamed. I am a woman.

I have children. Only one grew in my womb. It almost killed me to grow a child and give birth, but I had ended up pregnant—not intentionally—so there I was. It was my choice. I'd had miscarriages, and I'd decided to have a hysterectomy. Instead, the doctor told me there was a child in there. No one thought the pregnancy would last. Surgery, bed rest, other complications . . . but my child, like me, persisted. Another of my children was born to an opiate addict. Another of my children was born to a woman with addiction and mental health issues. None of the three children make me *more* of a woman. They do make me a mother.

I was a successful woman before motherhood.

It's all relative, still. I am who I am because of where I started, what I chose, and what I fight to be. I am a businesswoman. I am a mother. I am a sword fighter. I am a rock climber. I am a reader. I am a volunteer. We are all made up of the pieces of things imposed upon us and chosen by us. I am as defined by fists and rapes and disdain as I am by awards and swords and kids.

I am a woman, more than my womb, more than my roots. I strive not just for my children, but for my students, for my readers, and for the girls who are being told that they are limited.

You are limitless. You can survive. You can bloom.

Melissa Marr is a New York Times *bestselling, award-winning author of novels, picture books, and short fiction.*

JUST THE BEGINNING

By Jesselyn Silva

When I was seven years old, my dad took my brother and me to a boxing gym in Edgewater, New Jersey. It was boring to just sit and watch my dad train. He was having all the fun! So I decided I wanted to hit the bag, just like my dad. I begged him to let me put on a pair of gloves until he agreed. I started punching the bag like crazy right away. By the time I went to bed that night, I knew what I had a passion for: boxing!

As the years passed, I boxed more and more, but my classmates constantly told me that boxing is for boys only. This challenge motivated me more! Just like two-time Olympic gold medalist Claressa Shields said, if you ask a little boy who his five favorite boxers are, he will name five guys. My list isn't five guys, because it includes Claressa. And like Claressa, I want to break that boundary! God willing, I will be on a boy's top five list one day.

It's hard for female boxers to get on those lists, because we don't get the same attention the male boxers do. But that doesn't stop us. If anything, it means that girls and women are working harder than boys and men, because we don't have as many people supporting us. We have to bridge that distance on our own. One of my challenges is even finding girls to fight or spar with who are the right weight, age, and experience. Most girls have to fight that same girl over and over again. Fighting the same girl will help us both improve because we are still training and sharpening our boxing techniques, but being able to fight more girls with different boxing styles would better prepare me. You never know who you will step in the ring with, and you need to be ready for anything. For this reason, when I do spar, it's mostly with boys, but some boys are too embarrassed to spar with a girl. Also, their parents don't want to see their sons getting beaten up by a girl!

When I first started, most boys had the advantage, and some still do. But there was a time when a boy would come into the ring with a look on his face like I was easy work. I always showed him differently. Some parents even told their sons to go easy on me. I love when they underestimate me, though. It makes me want to go harder!

Every day in the gym is a challenge, from the drills to the push-ups, sit-ups, running, and pull-ups. But without all the hard work, I wouldn't be where I am today. I push myself a little more every day. I want to be great at anything I do! I know it will take a lot to get to where I want to be, and it took a lot to get to where I am now. Perseverance, hard work, and dedication got me here. I sacrificed time to get closer to my goals. And I can always count on support from my family, friends, coaches, and team. It's been four years since I started, and I've fallen in love with the process. I will continue to push myself to be a better Jesselyn than I was yesterday.

Every day I'm a step closer to my goals, and that alone helps keep me motivated. Other women who have come before me inspire me to keep moving. Like Barbara Buttrick, "the Mighty Atom." She was the first woman to have a fight broadcast on national television, which would be a big deal now but was an even bigger deal in 1954. Back then, it was not even normal for women to engage in sports in general. Barbara Buttrick and other female boxers have paved the way for me to showcase my talent to the world. I hope one day I can have all my fights televised for the whole world to see, and set an example for anyone who wants to reach their goals, no matter their gender.

But I haven't always been so sure about my path, and in a way, my first loss was another motivator for me. The girl was much taller, heavier, and older. She had done eleven fights and it was only my second. It hurt, because it felt as if all my hard work and dedication had not paid off. But I would not have done anything differently. I gave it my all that day. It was a loss on the books, but I gained the experience and that's important to me.

Other inspirations are my family and my teammates, because they have all played big roles on my road to success. Like my dad, for example—he's my number one fan. He has been there for me since the day I was born. After my first loss, my dad was the one who carried me out of that ring and let me cry in his arms. My teammates did the same; they treated me as if I had won the fight!

I have many goals, some bigger than others. I also have something called a "dream calendar." It helps me keep track of how many more days there are until my first major goal: the 2024 Olympics. I have to work so hard for this goal to be accomplished. I will have to go through trials, and if I win the trials, I'll go to the Olympics to compete against the best athletes in the world. I believe I can make it through and win the gold! Other dreams I have are to become a professional boxer, to win the World Boxing Council belt, and to be a Hall of Famer. As I have been saying, a lot of this takes hard work and dedication. You have to be very consistent. You can't go to the gym once a week. You have to go every day. Something that pushes me every day is something my grandfather told me: "When you have your first fight in Madison Square Garden, my spirit will be there right next to you, saying, 'Let's go!'" Sadly, he passed away two years ago from cancer. I love him and I believe he is going to be there for my first pro fight.

If you want to achieve something in life, go for it! Even if that means getting made fun of in school. Don't let anyone stop you, and don't let anyone say you can't. But most of all, never give up. I hope my story inspires you and encourages you to keep pushing for your goals. You, too, can be a breath of hope.

 Jesselyn Silva is a twelve-year-old boxer.

#NOFILTER

By Azure Antoinette

We were in sixth grade. It was February. My sister had just finished reading the life story of Malcolm X—she was inspired. I didn't understand his message—I gravitated toward Dr. King. We agreed to disagree. Her fist in the air, mine passively at my side, unfolded to an open palm.

My sister asked our teacher why we weren't celebrating Black History Month, and the teacher retorted:

"Why? We don't have a white history month."

It was 1993.

That was my life, though. Our mother—first-generation Portuguese black American—refused to let her two adopted black daughters (also mixed) be stereotypes. I am fairly certain that the word *stereotype* was etched into my vocabulary far before *cool* or *awesome*. Since I can remember, I have been hearing that I have to be prepared not only because I am a girl but paramountly because I am black. My mother, Octavia, demanded that we have phone presence that would dictate no indication of our race. So when I showed up for an interview, whoever was receiving me had the opportunity to be surprised by the presence of melanin in my skin tone. I followed suit. My mother was and is a brilliant orator, and I learned from the best. In some circles of the black race, we call this code-switching, and I became acutely adept at knowing just how to pivot for the audience and its pigment. By the time I reached high school, I was so disconnected from my heritage that I could barely recognize racism when it was slung in my actual face. It wasn't until I was twenty-six and heard a colleague refer to the spouse of a vendor as a "yard nigger" that I became so enraged at her guile and my personal ignorance. If it is possible to personally let down an entire race of people, I feel that my teenage years and early twenties were a direct disappointment to what it means to be black, a woman, an American.

Sophomore year of high school.

At the lockers, trying to fit in, although standing out as one of maybe six black students at my predominately white private school.

Junior class bully demanded I give her a piece of gum.

Told her I didn't have any more—spent the earlier class periods giving it out, even though being caught with it could have led to suspension.

She was angry that I refused.

Said, "Stupid nigger."

Slammed her locker shut.

My sister, with whom I rarely interacted in school, saw me upset and I told her what happened. She walked straight up to the junior and socked her in the face. My sister was suspended, pending my mother's visit to campus. She was then reinstated and the junior was sent home instead. No news media. No public address. Quiet. Silent.

1997.

The evening I heard the news of the acquittal of Trayvon Martin's murderer, I was in London. With my partner, who was white, Italian. Our good mutual friend, also white—Irish, I think.

They stayed quiet.

I remember feeling a knot in my stomach and throat.

The ache not just for the death of a black boy, but for just how little all my white world had to say about it.

I was on Facebook.

People were still just going on about their days.

Cat videos, vacation pics, et cetera.

Every so often, one of my righteous poet friends would post a photo in a hoodie, a rant on the trial, on American politics, and for the first time I started to hear murmurs about how Black Lives Matter. I thought—yes, they do.

Most of me didn't feel comfortable talking about my disgust with the verdict, with what seemed to be a corrupt system. And it made my partner uncomfortable, I could see it—I didn't want a divide in our household. We had enough to deal with. I remember telling her, *Your children will be half-black.* I remember she told me how excited that made her, that she always wanted biracial children. As far as raising a black son—we didn't spend too much time discussing it.

That was 2013.

It's 2016, June.

The symmetry between the hate speech and heinous racial crime and the amount of silence from my multiethnic friend group is just on the other side of terrifying. The latest tragedy: the massacre at Pulse, a gay nightclub in Orlando.

I am newly out of my almost-four-year relationship, engagement, to the person I thought was my forever. We ended for a myriad of reasons that will never fit in this essay. Needless to correspond, I am emotionally torn in ways I didn't imagine possible. Desperately pleading with a God I was hoping was still mine to kindly take me out of my misery. Instead, I continued to survive. When I woke to watch the news, see the terror for myself—she was the first person I contacted. I sat on the edge of my sister's couch and just cried my eyes out. I begged my ex to stay safe, wished blessings on her and her new girlfriend, and hung up the phone.

The part of my mind, or body, that was calm was beyond shock that this event had brought me to tears. It was as if I had lost a loved one. In essence, I had—many. But I've been an empath all my life. Why was this bringing me to my knees? The end of my fairy tale turned passive nightmare? I had been bisexual since college, not often public about it, but comfortable in my own skin for the most part. This wasn't an identity crisis.

Once I temporarily caught my breath, it became abhorrently clear.

All my "friends," my entire social media family, were silent.

No posting.

Not about Pulse.

Not about this epic loss of life.

And then it began.

One by one, Bible verses, scripture recitations about righteousness.

Then the media clips of pastors filled with hatred. My own mother, citing the passages that stated how unhappy God was with homosexuality. I felt like my heart was being ripped out of my chest all over again.

God didn't do that.

Not the God I call mine, not the one of love, not the one who says that human beings have no business, right, or jurisdiction to judge one another.

No, that God didn't do this.

I wrote a poem.

I recorded it live and posted it on YouTube.

My mother and I—we never discussed it.

Enter Alton Sterling.

Enter Philando Castile.

Enter live execution on Facebook.

Enter me, thirty-three years of age.

Black female American citizen strategizing with my black sister, black brother-in-law, black manager, about how we were all going to avoid driving in a car together. Because now Facebook, the place where people come together, was broadcasting live murders, and the state was giving the police officers who committed the crimes paid leave with tax dollars.

Social media exploded domestically.

Again, the silence on my feed was astounding. And the phrase returned.

Black Lives Matter.

Which was judiciously met with—ALL LIVES MATTER.

Then came the discord.

The pale faces that had no idea what it was like to be black in America started defending themselves, as if they were in a war that their skin tone was going to lose for them before they ever had the opportunity to fight.

People I thought I KNEW.

People I thought were my FRIENDS, justifying murder. Saying that black lives mattered but so did blue. I don't know when being pro-life as a black American started meaning that you hated cops. I don't know when it became okay to be silent or turn a blind eye to a father being shot in front of his daughter in the back seat of a car.

I don't know when it became so damn appealing for humans to just look ahead, band in solidarity, and wish me "love and light" in response to my ranting heartbreak online. When did my entire cadre of white people turn so ignorant? Or have these people always been that way? Was I secretly militant and never knew this about myself? Was I being selfish in feeling angry, hurt, frightened?

The amount of anger juxtaposed with the indecision that now was crushing my spirit was so heavy I could barely stand to look at my phone. Every day, a new comment or post about black sensitivity, and Facebook not being enjoyable anymore, and the incessant request for someone to break the dirge and please post some cat or dancing baby videos. I was sickened by the passive compassion I was surrounded by. Everywhere I looked and turned, there was some modicum of 1957, or of the uncivilized South. And my friends, my people, wanted to post recipes to their feeds.

What the fuck, America? What in the actual fuck is going on here?

What I know is this:

1. I stand out, because I do everything the wrong way and still manage to shine on a stage.
2. I am bisexual. Most think I can't make up my mind, or I'm confused. I am not. I am a devout purveyor of love. Whatever gender that comes in, I don't care.

3. I am a woman.

4. I am black.

On any day before this current melanin Armageddon, I was proud to tout those four facts. I wasn't uncomfortable—I was sufficient in whatever I was. Not from a stance of superior confidence, but because I had spent my entire life wanting people and things I couldn't have. I had gotten sick of chasing them, and so, as a result of exhaustion, I just sat down.

But right then, in 2016, all four of those facts—at least the last three—had me crying in public spaces, fearful of people who didn't look like me, and they had me publicly silent.

The summer of 2016 was the first time I understood the actual scent, texture, and nature of terrorism. As it is defined, it is to strike a deep sense of fear in a person or group of people. Mission accomplished. I stopped driving my car. Didn't leave my sister's apartment, and if I did, it was with someone who was white, who wasn't afraid to acknowledge that the country and its morals had gone to shit.

What breaks my heart to this day is the silence.

From the people I knew.

Still know.

Accepting these crimes as "a shame," hoping and praying and moving on by the next post.

To see those same quiet mouths now marching tirelessly, as the forty-fifth is a racist, hate-filled leader who not only dismisses people of color but loathes women. I see them posting—DAILY— and in tears as the country heads so far backward it makes you question if we ever progressed at all.

I see them aching about what they will tell their daughters.

I want to politely ask them to stop picketing, to sit down. And as for what to tell their daughters? I suppose they can finally side with Trayvon Martin's mother, Alton Sterling's partner. What am I supposed to tell my black son? That is, should I be foolish enough to give birth to him in these divided states of America.

 Azure Antoinette is a poet, an entrepreneur, and a millennial and arts education advocate.

I DIDN'T FIT IN—WHAT A GIFT

By Vicki Saunders

I grew up in a family full of male energy. I had three brothers and a mom and dad who were extremely competitive and ambitious. One of my brothers played in the NHL, another was drafted, another runs the family business, and we are all highly entrepreneurial and driven.

We grew up on a strawberry farm in the country outside Ottawa, Canada. We had thirty-two acres of pick-your-own strawberries at the time, and we kids and our friends worked tirelessly, weeding for hours and hours each week.

To get out of weeding, I played pretty much every sport I could find. I loved them all, but my favorites were ice hockey and soccer. I *loved* soccer. At that time, there were no girls' teams, so I played with the guys. When I was twelve years old, I was chosen to be on an all-star soccer team for a trip to the United States. The coach immediately said, "Um, that's not going to happen. We are traveling to the United States for a big tournament, and we can't have a girl on the bus with all the boys and rooming with boys' teams."

I didn't care that much about it, but one of my mom's friends was a mondo feminist (not that I knew what that was at the time) and lost it. She fought for me to be on the team. I was embarrassed. I didn't want anyone to make a big deal of it. She argued that it was totally unfair to exclude me, and that I deserved the position. She said that I had the skill and I should be recognized for it and I should step into it. I think the coaches were a bit worried about having to deal with a girl, so they were reluctant, but her convincing nature made their protest a nonstarter. And once they decided to make an exception for me, there was no turning back. I was very shy for most of my life and didn't want to stand out, but in this case I had no choice, with her advocating and pushing me to be part of the team.

So I found myself on a ten-hour bus ride to Washington, DC, with a team of twelve-year-old boys. I was aware that I was different, that the boys who didn't know me were not really on board with a girl on the team, and that the ones who did know me were not necessarily going to be my allies.

We started to play a card game called torture. It was brutal, hence the name: it involved the winner carrying out a series of physical punishments on the loser, with each punishment corresponding to a different card in the deck.

I won the game and started to go through the deck on the loser. A lot of the boys looked at me, wondering if I'd go through all the punishments. I didn't want them to think I wasn't up for it, so I went through the whole deck twice. I was a hit.

Later, as people were getting bored, someone suggested dropping lunch bags out the window onto passing cars. One of the boys dropped a bag that had a tomato or an apple in it. It hit a car's front grille and everyone exploded in surprise, giving kudos all round to the boy who had dropped it.

About thirty minutes later, our bus was pulled over and a police officer came on board. You've never heard a group of kids go silent so fast. The coach was told that something had been dropped out of the bus and caused damage to a car. The coach asked us if anyone knew anything about it. No one said a word. The coach slowly walked to the back of the bus, giving everyone the eye. He came right up to me and said, "Vicki, I know you won't lie. Did you see anything?"

I could feel everyone's eyes boring into me. What to do? I wanted to fit in. I had finally gained acceptance by being especially brutal to one of the kids in the game of torture. I felt sick to my stomach. I blushed immediately. I took a deep breath and said, "Nope, I didn't see anything." The coach looked at me long and hard, as did the police officer. It felt like an eternity. You could have heard a pin drop on the bus. The coach turned to the cop. They looked at each other. No one would tattle, so the cop left.

I sat back in my seat, heart racing. The boys looked at me. I was clearly a badass. I had earned their respect. But I felt terrible.

When we got to Washington, we met the team we were to be housed with. Each of us was to stay with someone from our host team.

The boy from the Washington-based team who was matched with me looked horrified, *I don't want to have a girl as my roommate* clearly written all over his face. He started to cry. It caused such a stir that they had to house another boy from my team with us so the Washington kid would agree to take me back to his house. I remember feeling upset by the whole thing. It was my first time away from home, and it made me realize for the first time that it was a boy's world and being a girl in it was a burden. The boys I hung out with in our small group in Canada treated me like one of them. But on this trip, as the only girl in a sea of boys, I had the first of what would be many experiences of what being the only girl on the team was like.

My whole life, I have been one of the only women in the room. I studied computer science and was one of the few women in class. I ran companies and was often the only woman on the panel at a conference or at the boardroom table. Though I didn't know it at the time, that first soccer experience signaled what my life was going to be like.

When I look back on it now, it also makes me mad that the coach used my status as the only girl to single me out and put me on the spot. I felt like I had to choose between being true to myself and fitting in. I chose fitting in at that moment, and in many other moments throughout my life. As I've gotten older and wiser, I have found ways to make sure I'm not put in a situation that makes me compromise who I am. For too long, women have had to play in a man's world, by men's rules. Thankfully, that's changing now. Women's innovations and women's perspectives are needed now more than ever as the world is being redesigned to work for all of us, not just 50 percent of the population. Always remember that you don't have to fit into a world that doesn't feel right. You can go and create your own world without sacrificing who you are, which is just what I'm doing now.

 Vicki Saunders is an entrepreneur, an award-winning mentor, and the founder of SheEO.

WINDOW SEAT

By Representative Leslie Herod

Growing up, I was enamored with TV families, especially those that featured young girls my age. They had huge, cool rooms with bright, hip decor. And they all had window seats.

For me, the window seats were a sign of stability—and offered literal windows into a world that wasn't mine, one that I coveted. There was always a mom and a dad, usually an annoying but lovable sibling, and a best friend who would climb in through that window and bring unwavering support and entertaining hijinks. When the girl got into trouble, there was usually some overarching life lesson—a teachable moment—and the family would all come together to decide on a punishment, hug, and remind her that no matter what, they were a family and she was always loved.

My reality was much different from those of the window-seat kids. My family was a distant family. My dad had left long before, leaving only my mother, my brother, and me. When we weren't fighting, my mother was battling her addiction or off to a stint in rehab. I also had an older sister, but she had been in jail for most of my youth and was more of a warning of what my life could become than a role model. For us, hijinks could get you locked up.

I didn't want that. I didn't want to be like my sister or my mom, so I would prop up my pillows near the closest window and read. My own makeshift window seat, and my best way to find a few moments of escape. I read everything. From the Baby-Sitters Club and R. L. Stine to the *Encyclopaedia Britannica*. Reading allowed me to disappear entirely into another world. Into a life of opportunity.

To be clear, I never felt sorry for myself. There was never time for that. It was my job to hold the family together as my mother's addiction and depression worsened. Not many of my friends really knew what my life was like at home. They saw a well-read, polite young lady and thought I was a model child.

The cracks started to show around middle school. People wondered where my mom was. As I won all these accolades for my grades, danced in competitions, and even sang (very poorly) in talent shows, she never could bring herself to show up.

For a while, I was okay with that. It was just how we were. My mom worked hard, was an officer in the military, and did her best to make a better life for my brother and me. I treasured time at home with her, when we gave each other belly laughs while she was getting ready for a glamorous evening on the town. I loved and admired her. Looking back, I realize how hard it must have been for her. To be a black woman, a single mother, having grown up in Oakland in the 1960s. Her path was not easy. She had two options: be strong or perish. It is no surprise that she turned to alcohol and prescription drugs to deal with it all, while the weight of keeping the family intact fell on my shoulders.

Something changed when I got into high school. Perhaps it was hormones, perhaps it was something else, but I became sick of it all. Tired of playing mom and pretending to be that perfect window-seat family, I decided to do things differently.

I stopped making excuses for my mother. I stopped trying to do things that would win me recognition—I didn't see the point. In my mind, nothing I did would change my life—or make her show up. So I started skipping classes, getting into fights at school, and doing what I wanted. My grades slipped (though not much, thankfully, as my curious and studious childhood made school pretty easy for me). Teachers and counselors questioned whether I would get pregnant or drop out of school altogether. Rather than being exceptional, I became a statistic: another black teen from a broken family who had little chance of success. I was falling. It felt as though no one around me noticed or cared. I'm not sure I did either.

But through all this, there was always a safe space to land, whether I realized it or not: the dreams of a young girl who knew that a better view was out there, if only she could find the right window seat.

As I approached rock bottom, two people reached out their hands to me, offered me that seat, and refused to give up. Their names were John and Kathy, and they gave me their entire family. They were the parents of one of my closest friends, Madonia. Theirs was a new family, with stepparents and stepsiblings, but no one called each other *step,* just brother and sister and mom and dad. As a family, they were just figuring it all out. Not perfect, but real. Flawed and loving. They took me in as their own and reminded me of who I could become.

I still remember when John and Kathy sat me down for a talk.

It was awkward. I was around sixteen and had been in and out of my mom's house countless times, and my brother was usually not far behind. I was very worried they would tell me that I was coming around too much. Instead, they set boundaries for me. I was always welcome in their house, but I had to go to school and make curfew. I had to tell them when I was going to be late or if my plans changed.

John told me that I reminded him of one of his favorite songs: "Black Butterfly" by Deniece Williams.

> *Morning light, silken dream take flight*
> *As the darkness gives way to the dawn*
> *You survived, now your moment has arrived*
> *Now your dream has finally been born*
> *Black Butterfly, sail across the waters*
> *Tell your sons and daughters what the struggle brings*
> *Black Butterfly, set the skies on fire*
> *Rise up even higher*
> *So the ageless winds of time can catch your wings*

For what felt like the first time in my life, I felt seen and wholly loved. At the end of the conversation, they put their arms around me, called me their daughter, and gave me a house key.

In that moment, I realized that I had a window seat, if only a figurative one, at least for a while. It was different, of course, from the ones I saw on TV. It didn't matter, though, because I was home.

Perhaps it was at that moment, somewhere in my still-young brain, that I decided I would someday help others, just as John and Kathy had helped me. Help folks see that they don't have to go through this world alone. The burdens of life and family can certainly feel overwhelming at times, but there is no shame in getting help—no matter your age or station in life. I certainly didn't know I would one day turn my window-seat dream into a legislative seat in the state capitol—but I knew that I could go places and that I wouldn't go there alone.

Being sworn in as the first openly LGBT African American person to serve in the Colorado legislature was a powerful moment. As I looked up into the House gallery, I saw the family that I had created over the years. A village: friends from all over. And though my mom didn't make it to my swearing-in, John and Kathy were there, as was the rest of their family, and my brother. As I looked up at them from my seat on the House floor, I knew they were proud and I was loved.

While I don't have an actual window seat yet, I wouldn't trade that view for anything in the world.

 Representative Leslie Herod is the first African American LGBT candidate elected to Colorado's state legislature, representing northeast Denver in the House of Representatives.

REFLECTIONS OF A YOUNGER SILVERCLOUD

By Johnny Silvercloud

Since I grew up in a predominantly Afro-American location, I have a hard time remembering dealing with racism as a child.

I think part of the difficulty stems from the fact that, technically, it's easy to internalize racism as a whole. White supremacy is like the default apps you get on your iPhone; you have to be aware of an alternate set of programs in order to question the existence of the things you are given by default. I was not truly aware of much until I was an adult.

EARLIEST MEMORY OF INTERNALIZED RACISM

I remember one time when I was in the fourth grade. This was at Charles Young Elementary School, in northeast Washington, DC. It was a hot day, the kind that spring gives you on the edge of summer. While DC usually has the type of humidity that imitates swamp life, it was dry that day.

The grass outside at the designated play area was patchy like my drunken uncle Leonard's head, may he rest in peace. Strangely enough, the dirt kicked up in the air and gave the area a sepia tint. I do not remember too much, but I do remember talking to some kid, black like me. I do not remember the details, but I remember the solid portion: the kid said something about why I did not curse. I asked him why he cursed and swore. In short, he said that he figured that he was not going to amount to much in life. At the time, I did not know exactly what he meant, but I sure enough did not agree with his reasoning. As an adult, I can clearly see that he had internalized racism. American media demonized young black children back then in the same manner they do now. He was clearly exposed to the totality of a society that crushes the spirit of black people. This includes children. Persistent negative depictions of black people suggest that that is all it's possible to amount to. If he was never going to amount to anything, why did it matter if he swore?

SAYING NO

It was the late 1990s, and I was in high school. My life had expanded out into Maryland by this time, still not far from DC. We called it PG County—it was just like Washington, but with more trees and greener grass. In my first year of high school, I remember this one person, black like me, asking me if I smoked weed. I told him I did not, and he was surprised. He said that I would smoke weed before I graduated from high school. Not only did I never smoke weed in high school, but I have still never smoked weed.

For some strange reason, I had an inexplicable, immense dislike of adhering to predetermined negative expectations, especially those based on race. I do not remember how this was built in me. To me, this was a straight-from-the-gut response, perhaps an instinct. I disliked the notion so much, not only did I "say no to drugs" in high school, I took it even further—I've never smoked weed in my life. Someone saying I'm going to smoke weed just because I'm black? I don't think so. You can say no, too. Not only can you say no to drugs, you can say no to internalized racism.

TRUEST THOUGHT I EVER HAD

The interesting thing about being in Maryland as a teenager was the exposure to white kids. By then, I had been in many fights, most with folks who were hoping I was a stereotypical nerd. I was not physically intimidating. I was skinny, not exactly the most athletic, and I liked the notion that people saw just a nerd; I enjoyed being a surprise. In Maryland, however, dealing with white ignorance was fascinating. I couldn't just fight my way through bullies like I used to. I had to use my mind.

In the white space of Laurel, Maryland, I was stereotyped differently. One white teen named Brad said something about how I didn't seem that intimidating, for a black teen. I pointed out that a smart black child is actually *more* terrifying to many than a dumb one. I don't exactly know why, but that's how it is. White people do not like intelligent black people, who do not tend toward aiding white supremacy. White people seem to fear and hate those of us who use our minds to tear the system of white supremacy down. The fear due to my intellectual capacity is more terrifying than the physicality of my fists by far, even now, when I'm more physically intimidating. One great mind is worth more than a thousand great fists.

WHITE PEOPLE THINKING YOU'RE STUPID

One thing I always hate is when people think I am stupid because I am black. White kids loved assuming such things. This was never based on any actual academic matters—it was just the way

181

I talked, on top of my skin color. It made me want to be three times better than them in everything we did. Sometimes besting them in the classroom wasn't enough—I wanted to hurt them physically. I wanted to immediately make them feel pain. Some did get punched, but only when I was provoked, cornered. I had no patience for bullies. I would not recommend too much fighting, however; laws are far stricter these days, and white supremacy enjoys placing nonwhite children into the prison-industrial complex. Worse is the internet deal these days, and that is going to only get worse.

WHEN SEX AND RACE INTERSECT

I remember my school having exchange students. They seemed to always come from the Eurasian landmass. I remember this one girl, blond, from one of the Germanic countries. I forgot her name, but I have not ever forgotten how she used to look at me.

I had no idea how to handle this. I mean, I knew she was good-looking. But what? Talking to the foreign white girl? How would that be possible? At least to my knowledge, no other white girl was looking at me like that. Despite the school being a roughly fifty-fifty mix of white and nonwhite, it seemed like the race line concerning intimate relationships was solidly there. Did I talk to her? Say anything? Pass a "Like me?" note? Nope. Nothing. Total paralysis.

Upon further experience and study, I have realized that as a foreign white person, she wasn't white like American whites are. When European people say they are white, it's just a mere description, but when American white people say it, it means they are boss. There's a difference. Many American whites do not even like to mention they are white at all, because it points to their privilege.

This difference in racial attitudes comes from the American institution of slavery. While Europeans had slavery, they did not place emphasis on separating races, as American whites did with their slave codes. Americans sought to separate blacks from everyone else, because in order to do what they did to us—breed us just for slavery, sell us off, separate us from family like horses or dogs, whip us, beat us, mutilate us, rape us, lynch us, keep us in a constant state of fear and terror—they had to dehumanize us in a way that probably has never otherwise been seen in world history. White supremacy in America didn't like the notion of races mixing either. So there had to be an extra level of dehumanization—demonization, if you will—placed upon black people to make us infinitely undesirable. European whites didn't take all these extra dehumanization measures to subtract from black people's humanity, as American whites did.

One must also look at the creation of the notion of being "white." While Europeans were aware that they looked different from the original natives of those foreign lands they explored and sought to plunder, the notion of being white is an American thing. The notion of being white came from separating Amerindians from whites. The Europeans in the New World invented the concept of whiteness in order to decide who got the most resources. American whites, though, felt that there was a sense of purity in their existence. American whites drew parallels between whiteness and godliness, and blackness and evil. This is why race and sex intertwine with each other: whites fear that they will be eradicated if they are mixed with black people. So there were laws and sentiments constructed here that Europe didn't exactly have. The effects of slavery still linger.

Anyway, that Germanic girl did not have the racial fear of

black boys that American white girls did. I couldn't really grasp that back then, her seemingly brash behavior. I would later explore this further when I graduated from high school, joined the armed forces, and was stationed in Germany at the age of nineteen.

CLOSURE

Overall, racism is something that governs every aspect of life in America. Racism still decides which communities get which resources. Racism still decides whom a police officer can murder with impunity. Honestly, I cannot say that racism will be eradicated before I die. But that doesn't mean that one shouldn't fight for what's right, fight for what is just. In America, as racist as this nation is, a person of color just juggles double consciousness—the self that you display because of white fragility concerning race relations, and your actual Self, who knows there's an inherent racial problem in all layers of society. Never doubt your senses. Never doubt your true Self.

 Johnny Silvercloud is an abolitionist photographer, writer, and speaker who cares deeply about the self-care of people of color, especially black folks.

SOMETIMES YOU ARE BETTER OFF NOT KNOWING

By Binta Niambi Brown

He laced his long, manicured fingers behind his head, crossed his black-cashmere-socked feet on his desk, leaned back in his executive chair, and stared at me. I'd worked for him for a year, had been to his home for department gatherings, but until the day he called me into his office, we had never spoken, never interacted. So many times we had passed one another in hallways, and yet this was the first time he seemed aware I existed, or that I worked for him.

We sat in his office, which smelled faintly of leather and high-quality tobacco, with two other witnesses. One had claimed to many that I was his star, his ace, the future of the firm, a shining example to others. Then he spoke.

"We don't believe that your kind of people are cut out for this kind of work. Your people should do other things—less complex, sophisticated, cerebral things. Perhaps you should try something else."

There may have been other words spoken, but those are the

only words I remember hearing. *Your kind of people. This kind of work. NO.*

My advocate did not advocate. The other witness did not look me in the eye. Time stopped. My body froze. My face hurt from working so hard to maintain my composure, my sanity, my professionalism. *Hold it together, hold it together,* I told myself. *You did not hear him correctly. That is not what he meant. It could not be.*

I left his office, passed my desk, headed straight out the door, went home, and cried, and cried, and cried. My life, I thought, was over . . . at twenty-three. Before I'd had a chance to even start living, doing, creating. My hopes, my dreams, my belief in myself . . . all temporarily dashed. My esteem . . . diminished.

For that brief moment in time, that no, that rejection based only on my immutable characteristics and not on my true potential or achievement, echoed loudly and repeatedly in my head, filling up all space, reverberating and causing me to forget temporarily who I was, what I believed, and where I came from. Then I remembered.

This was the first time I'd literally heard no, but it was most certainly not the first time someone had said no to me. In fact, at virtually every turn, someone has asserted, *No, no, you can't*—confusing actual ability with perception rooted in stereotype or bias. My young life, in retrospect, was a litany of no.

I grew up in the South, in a community where the main roads and rival high schools were named after Jefferson Davis, the failed president of the failed idea of the Confederacy, and his Confederate generals, Robert E. Lee and J. E. B. Stuart—each of them men who fought in support of a cause dedicated to maintaining an economic system that debased, dehumanized, and denied the dignity of human beings. Men whose sons and daughters feared and would fight against the integration of black people into schools, churches, neighborhoods, jobs, and society.

I grew up in a place that celebrated figures whose mission in life was to deny the humanity of people like me, and yet I was never affected by that history, perhaps because I was also born in the shadow of the civil rights movement, to parents who did not allow me the luxury of deeming myself oppressed or, worse, inferior. So I didn't know and didn't learn that by virtue of gender or race, or the combination of the wrong gender and the wrong race, the world might somehow see me as less than. Consequently, when I was a girl, I never really noticed my gender—or, for that matter, my race. And I never, ever thought of myself as somehow inferior to or different from anyone else.

I am a descendant of slaves; however, I was born free, and fundamental to that freedom was the freedom to refuse to be limited by the racist legacy of the environment in which I grew up.

Yet the vestiges of that past were everywhere. Menacing, lurking, attempting to hold me back on the one hand, strengthening my muscles of resistance and resilience from a very young age on the other.

My eighth-grade English teacher, perhaps unaware that legalized segregation had ended, insisted I sit in the back of the classroom, refused to call on me when I raised my hand, accused me of having others write my papers (claiming that I was not capable intellectually of writing with sophistication), and routinely gave me lower marks (insisting that I did not participate in class and was never prepared). She also said I was not smart enough for her class and petitioned to have me removed.

I refused to let her perspective diminish my curiosity, my love of reading, or my need to express myself through writing.

Instead, I allowed myself to become lost in the worlds of the texts she assigned, books that opened new frontiers, expanding my imagination, my sense of the possible, and my sense of self. I became a reader who refused to stop reading, a writer who refused to stop writing . . . encouraged by the doors each activity opened for me. I found freedom in my study and would not be limited.

My high school guidance counselor told me not to apply to Ivy League schools and elite conservatories, to ignore their various recruitment efforts, saying that, no, I would not be admitted, and that even if I did somehow manage admission, I would not be able to survive academically or socially at those schools. If I got in, he claimed, I would fail out. I would be better off going to a lower-tier state college, where I could handle the course load and where I would have more black classmates.

It seemed irrelevant to him that I had been taking honors courses throughout high school and that, having overcome teachers who were confused by my presence in all-white classes, I regularly earned high marks and high test scores. And though at sixteen I'd performed around the world in elite youth symphony orchestras, the idea of a black classical musician apparently confounded him (as it did many: *No, your kind of people do not play this kind of music*). In his world, since he had not seen black symphonic musicians, it was not possible to become one.

I applied to an elite school, Barnard College, and an elite conservatory, Manhattan School of Music, gained admission to both, initially enrolled in both, graduated from Barnard with honors in multiple areas of study, and gained admission to and attended Columbia Law School. Though one man sought to limit me, I never allowed myself the luxury of believing or subscribing to his perspective. My intellectual curiosity, self-belief, passion, purpose, and drive to work on behalf of others and build a better society were simply too insatiable to be limited by his narrow, reductionist perspective.

So much of my life has been a litany of no, and yet no had never, ever stopped me, paralyzed me. Never before had I felt shackled by the indifference of others, or by their assertion of who I was or who I could be. Instead, I'd always persisted in the face of bias, and in some cases overt antagonism, relentless in my refusal to become enslaved by the soft bigotry of low expectations and the overt racism of those who'd not yet evolved into the fullness of their own humanity.

Each no became an opportunity, a lesson that opened new doors and new experiences, beckoning me to walk through them, to discover, to lead and build. Sometimes the noes operated as a pleasant challenge that would prepare me to refuse to quit, to refuse to give up or give in—particularly when the cause was the faithlessness, jealousy, or hatred of another person.

I learned to laugh at the folly of certain adults and to trust in the guidance of those—namely, my parents, grandparents, aunts, and uncles—who imbued me with a fearlessness rooted in faith. They raised me to believe that with hard work, discipline, passion, and a commitment to inquiry and excellence, I could do and achieve whatever I wanted. They also raised me with a deep and resilient faith that became my own, buoying me in times of darkness and struggle, teaching me to trust in things bigger than the whimsy of humanity.

No, you can't did not exist in my world.

Until that day, sitting in that man's office, when my childhood innocence was shattered and my dreams were threatened. It was the first time I felt the sting of no, the first time my determination was genuinely threatened. This sting became a turning point, not because I acquiesced—although I was so tempted—but because it jarred me into an awareness that compelled a choice: define myself by his narrow perspective and become enslaved by a certain kind of complacency, or rise above it and achieve in a way that opens up paths for more people, creating platforms for the advancement and potential of all human beings that resist any effort to debase or delimit the dignity of any person or community. I became aware that if I stopped, if I gave up, others might also quit, or perhaps not even try to live up to their potential. I could unwind my freedom by embracing a false narrative, or instead I could choose love and be love in the world.

The consequence of refusing to acquiesce, of walking through a door that bigotry opened, was that I found in that firm, in that place, exceptional mentors, guides, and teachers. These men and women became dear friends who have believed in me and shaped my career ever since, ensuring my ability to achieve my greatest heights, to never stop believing in my capacity, regardless of the darkness that might lurk within the hearts of some. These guides enabled me to see and trust the goodness inherent in many.

It is love that caused me to triumph over indignity and hurt, and it is love—love of self, love of the other, love of humanity, and love of freedom—that has motivated every action since. If we are love, and exist in love and determination, we can transcend the fear at the root of no.

 Binta Niambi Brown is a business leader in the music industry and the founder of Big Mouth Records.

HOW WRITING A COLLEGE ESSAY TAUGHT ME MORE ABOUT MYSELF THAN LIFE

By Patricia Valoy

When I was applying to colleges, there was only one place I wanted to attend: Columbia University's school of engineering. Columbia is an Ivy League school, one of the most prestigious universities in the world, but I didn't know this at the time. I just knew it had the program I wanted and was close enough to my family that I could visit on weekends. I was so focused on this school that I would tell people I was not going to apply to any other, which resulted in horrified gasps and sometimes a chuckle.

But I had a reason for this tenacity. I wasn't trying to be a proud teen defying all conventions (though there was some naïveté in my actions). I just wanted to feel in control of my future, and that I was capable of the things that I saw only in movies and on TV shows, where teens always seemed to apply to their dream schools and get in.

My teen years felt unremarkable as I lived them. I don't think of them as negative, but I do associate so many of those years with pain and growing up too fast. My parents separated when

I was twelve years old, and from then on I was coparent to my younger sisters alongside my now-single mom. The separation removed us from a violent living situation but left us vulnerable in other ways, in desperate need of resources, from the most basic necessities like food and housing to less talked-about (but just as vital) things like access to mental health counseling. We lived in a neighborhood that was underserved and decaying from poverty, drugs, and police violence. It felt isolated and depleted of resources and possibilities. Most of the adults I knew were living under the poverty line and working nonstop just to put food on the table. I didn't know any professionals besides my schoolteachers, and the other jobs available for a girl like me (like hairdresser and retail clerk) were not to my liking. It felt as if the only way to move ahead was to aim for the stars, because there was nothing else within reach anyway.

I learned early on that people depended on me. I would never have the luxury of messing up, of not succeeding, or of living off my parents. My mother expected me to be self-sufficient soon after high school and to help out monetarily when I was able. She wasn't trying to put unrealistic expectations on me, but I was the only person she could be vulnerable with and ask for financial support from. Perhaps she shouldn't have put such a burden on me, but the reality is that she always knew I was capable of it, and had I failed, she would have been there for me, as proud as ever.

Early on, I internalized the trope that education is the way to salvation. While I understand now that education does not have all the answers, I had no other choice as a teenager. I needed to use the only part of myself I alone could control: my brain. I devoured books, volunteered for all school activities, and poured my energy into studying for tests and doing homework. I was every teacher's model student, and I would be lying if I said I didn't love this attention.

So I started to apply to college and was immediately consumed by the process. The application was long and tedious, and as I filled it out, I felt that perhaps I wasn't really as great as I'd thought. I learned that test scores and extracurricular activities were important, but most significant was my essay. I needed to make a first impression, to capture the admissions officers with my words, to find a way to let them into my world so that they could get to know me as a person. But as great as I was at math and science, and as much as I loved reading and discussing literature, I hated writing and didn't feel that it was my forte.

I agonized over it for weeks and finally settled on what I thought was a brilliant idea. I would write an unconventional essay by creating a fictional dialogue between me and an admissions officer. I felt that this was an imaginative way for the admissions staff to know the answers I would give to their imagined questions. So off I went to write the worst thing I've ever written.

And I felt proud of it. I thought it was innovative! When a guidance counselor known for his tough love told me that he would be willing to review my college essay, I jumped at the idea. I printed it, wrote a note on a Post-it, and left it on his desk.

A few hours later he found me walking down the hallway and invited me to his office to discuss the essay. As soon as I sat down, he told me how disappointed he was in me for not taking the process seriously. He said he had never seen anything so poorly written and even went so far as to claim he couldn't finish reading it. I wanted to cry, but I held my composure. He asked where I was planning on applying, and when I said Columbia, he nearly fell off his chair. I had to sit through an entire monologue about how the Ivy League works and how little chance I had of getting in. He said my grades were good, but not nearly good enough for the curriculum at Columbia, not to mention the cost of attending, and the fact that I was about to graduate from a high school in the most underserved neighborhood in New York City. My school had no calculus or physics teachers and didn't even offer AP courses. I know now that he wanted to give me a reality check, but it felt like I was being told I was not worthy.

So I went home and cried. And then I decided to prove him wrong.

He had given me the best topic for my essay. Who could resist a story of a tenacious Latina girl living in the ghetto, surrounded by people who didn't believe she could achieve the impossible? I wasn't into tokenizing myself, but if that was going to get me into Columbia, I was going to have to swallow my pride and give them what they wanted. I also realized I needed better college prep and support, so I asked around and found a local organization that offered these services.

As I walked through the door of College Steps in Brooklyn, I was greeted warmly by a person who treated me like an individual rather than just another naïve student who was probably in over her head. I told her I wanted to attend Columbia, and instead of scoffing, she said she would do her best to help. She edited my essay several times, reviewed my application, and explained to me the need to apply to other schools just in case. She helped me research schools that I would love just as much as Columbia. We worked on my interview skills and talked about what to expect if I got accepted—and what would happen if I didn't. She also helped with my financial aid application and encouraged me to apply for scholarships.

And guess what. I did get into Columbia's engineering school, and I got a nearly full scholarship to attend.

Thirteen years later, I am still in touch with my counselor from College Steps, Jennifer Cabán. She is my friend and my mentor, but even more than that, she taught me how to turn my dreams into tangible steps that I could take to get to the stars.

I often wonder how my life would be if I hadn't been accepted to my dream school. I treasure my time at Columbia, and I am thankful that at such a young age I knew what I wanted—but had I not been accepted, I would have learned to love another school. There would have been other lessons for me, and I would have adjusted and adapted. But I am forever grateful for the opportunities that I was granted. As a teen, I existed between a child's protected world and an uncertain future. It's no wonder I created dreams for myself that felt almost impossible. But impossible is also the beginning of every great story, and while I don't want to live through my teen years again, I look back at them fondly and sometimes wish I could bring a little spark of teen me into my adult life. Teen me was made of Teflon.

 Patricia Valoy is a feminist activist, consultant, writer, and speaker on diversity and gender in science, technology, engineering, and math.

NEVERTHELESS, I WRITE

By Amy Fox

The occupational therapist waves the ultrasound wand over my forearm, and I feel a slight prickle. Across the table sits a woman whose arm is held together by a suspension bridge of pins and rubber bands. She had a rollerblading accident. A few feet away, my father reads his newspaper. The therapist addresses my fears about whether I will be able to type or write by hand again. She thinks I am going to heal completely. And if I don't? She says, rather cheerily, that there are lots of jobs out there that don't require writing.

There is a pause. I hear her words but I can't respond to them. Perhaps they have been spoken to someone else. My dad rustles his newspaper.

"She wants to be a writer," he says.

I don't remember how the occupational therapist responded. She did not mention voice dictation software, which I am using to dictate this essay twenty-one years later. The software was not yet available, and I don't think any of us could have imagined it would make my future life as a writer possible.

I was nineteen years old. I did not have an arm held together by pins. My wrists looked remarkably normal. They gave no indication of the tendinitis inflaming them from within. I did not have a spectacular accident, did not tumble off Rollerblades. I stayed up too many nights hunched over a computer, typing college papers. And then I took a summer job as a medical file clerk. All day long I slid manila folders into their proper places. If I see someone bend a wrist in just that way now, my stomach flip-flops.

I have received various diagnoses for what happened to me that summer. Mostly they fall under the category of repetitive strain injury, or RSI, damage done by repetitive motions like, in my case, typing and filing. These are sneaky injuries—largely invisible. There are many factors that can make one prone to RSI and can explain why some people develop inflammation from office work while others do not.

Most of the women working in that hospital file room were experiencing some form of RSI. Many of my coworkers wore wrist splints. One day the hospital sent someone from HR to talk to us about the hidden risks of our mundane work. She advocated taking stretch breaks. My coworkers spoke up. We had quotas—expectations of how many folders we should file per hour—and we would not make these quotas if we took breaks. The HR consultant assured us our manager would work with us to address this discrepancy. And then she left the room and there was never another word about it. The quotas remained.

For most of those women, this was full-time, ongoing employment. I knew I was lucky. It was a summer job for me, a way for me to help pay for college. And perhaps that is why my parents and I believed that there was no way this job would have a lasting impact on my body. I did see a doctor, who assured me

I was young and healthy and the tendinitis would heal. He was wrong. In some people, RSI can become chronic. By the end of the summer, my symptoms had increased, I was seeing the occupational therapist, and she was assuring me I could have a future that would not involve writing.

When I returned to college that September, typing was one of many things I could not do. I could not lift heavy things or open heavy doors. Even carrying my tray in the cafeteria was painful.

I relied heavily on my roommate for everyday tasks. I registered with the college as a student with a disability under the Americans with Disabilities Act, which enabled me to have a note taker and typist to help me complete my work.

I began this essay wanting to write about being young and female, but somehow I find myself writing about being disabled. And yet it is truly in the intersection of these identities that I have come to understand my experience of becoming no longer able-bodied.

I was a people pleaser, like so many young women, and I never wanted to inconvenience anyone. I had always hated asking for help and had prided myself on my self-sufficiency. But now I had to rely on others to get me through the day, and I saw that as a personal failure.

I found it especially difficult to ask for help when my injuries were invisible and somewhat mysterious. Doctors in 1995 were just beginning to understand RSI and chronic pain. There was a tendency to dismiss symptoms, particularly in women. One hand specialist I saw told my father that my symptoms were entirely psychological. Although we later found other doctors to refute this, that hand specialist's words lingered in my head. I didn't know anything about the historical context of doctors not taking women's health complaints seriously. All I knew was that this man believed I was making this up. I began to fear that others thought the same thing, and it turned out that some of them did. One day my roommate, my closest friend, who would button my shirt for me if that action was too painful, told me that some people believed my injuries made no sense, and she asked if I was faking them.

When I think about my persistence during this time, I don't think of being brave or strong. I moved forward and kept up with my academic work because I did not know what else to do. But I was consumed with self-doubt. I didn't know how to advocate for myself, for my right to be listened to by a doctor, to receive good medical care, to be treated well by someone who called herself my friend. I did not fundamentally believe that I was worth the fuss or the resources it took to keep me functioning. That summer when my symptoms first appeared, my grandmother had told me to quit the filing job. She said no job was worth hurting myself. But the truth is that I didn't believe her. I thought it was more important to make the money I had promised my parents I would make, to be a good girl and do as I was told, by my manager, by my doctor, by all those around me. And if a doctor and a friend did not believe I was in pain, who was I to question them?

That difficult school year was also the year I took my first playwriting class. I had written stories and acted since childhood, and suddenly I discovered I could combine these two loves. With the help of my assigned typist, I managed to complete the class. Sensing my newfound passion, my professor recommended that I attend a summer theater workshop at Vassar College.

I was thrilled at the idea of spending a summer immersed in playwriting. But when I arrived at Vassar, I was terrified. I had not told anyone about my physical limitations. I still did not want to ask for help, to seem like I needed special treatment. My heart sank as I read the schedule. Daily playwriting classes in the mornings. In the evenings we would work as assistants to professional playwrights and backstage crews on shows. Not only did I not know how I would complete the writing itself, I was in no shape to be anyone's assistant or to hoist curtains. I imagined myself trying to explain this and coming off as some entitled young woman who didn't want to get her normal-looking hands dirty.

In our first writing workshop, the teacher announced the class would consist of longhand writing exercises and that each night we would type up scenes to be read the next morning. At the break I took her aside and explained that I would not be able to continue the program. I would probably have to go home. She took one look at me and said: Of course you will continue. It was a no-brainer for her. She told me to get a tape recorder and record my freewriting. When the rest of the class returned, she told us we were a community, there to support each other, and announced that she expected them to take turns typing for me every night. To my shock, nobody blinked at this. Nobody questioned it. The other students in that class are still some of my dearest friends. When I told them what had happened with my college roommate, they were in complete shock. The idea that a friend would doubt and question and ultimately abandon a friend in need simply did not compute for them. Those classmates taught me what friendship could look like.

I still battle with RSI and chronic pain. These days I dictate everything I write to voice software. The technology has allowed me to pursue a career as a screenwriter and playwright. I also teach writing, and I recognize that I have the power to influence not only how young people feel about their writing, but how they feel about themselves. Too often, our society tells us that our most vulnerable are not worth fighting for. My playwriting teacher was not interested in the limitations of my body. She was interested in my mind, my stories, and what I had to say. And her belief in the importance of my voice changed how I saw myself.

As I revise these words, my right wrist begins to ache. But I've got a story to tell, so I'm going to keep writing.

 Amy Fox is an acclaimed screenwriter, playwright, and educator and a passionate advocate for elevating women's voices in the arts and the workplace.

THE NEW KID

By José Antonio Tijerino

As I stepped off the warm, still-exhaling plane from Managua, Nicaragua, to Washington, DC, I did so with great uneasiness, not excitement. I was six years old and had left my friends, my beloved *abuelita,* the comfort of year-round tropical weather, delicious *pan dulce,* and a colorful landscape of volcanoes, lakes, and beaches for the monochromatic, gray-city schemes of pavement, buildings, and serious men in suits. At least that's what I saw on the taxi ride from the airport to our new home in America.

I woke up the very next morning to my first day of first grade. It was a jarring adjustment; I had never gone to kindergarten, and I spoke only Spanish. I felt isolated among the other children, who looked like characters from pictures in books I had flipped through back at my old home. The teachers couldn't even say my name right, so they simply took a stab at it and moved on. I didn't say a word the entire year, but that didn't matter. No one would have understood me, and besides, no one tried to talk to me. I had to repeat first grade, and teachers and other children treated me as if I was stupid, invisible, or from another planet. No, I was from Nicaragua.

But I survived and adjusted. And ten years passed.

Most summers, my family visited Nicaragua to see my *abuelita*, cousins, and friends, except now I felt as though I didn't really belong there—the way I had felt when I first landed in the United States. Kids I had grown up with made fun of my Spanish, which had flip-flopped into being my second language. They made fun of my clothes, the music I listened to, my hairstyle, even more hostilely than the kids in DC had when I had tried to fit in in the United States. I felt judged, as if I was auditioning for them on a reality show. Add to the mix an early-teen shyness around girls that I disguised as cool aloofness, paired with a simmering, newly appended angst, and it seemed the entire summer was going to explode. And then it did.

Boom! Homemade bombs ripped through venues I had just been to. *Pop, pop, pop!* Gunfire sounded like the Fourth of July, except the spectacle was in the streets, not in the sky. Rampant kidnappings swept through neighborhoods as many kids I grew up with were sent to the front lines of an impending civil war. Lying facedown on the cool, smooth linoleum became comforting as we heard the cacophonous mayhem swirling just outside my grandmother's house. The catalyst was the assassination of the editor of an antigovernment newspaper, and many blamed the Nicaraguan president for the murder. This was an opening for the revolutionaries to set in motion a brutal rebellion against the government's military, and I watched a scene in a political-upheaval thriller unfold in real time, with the entire country as the movie screen. My beloved Nicaragua was on the cusp of civil war, and everyone, it seemed, was choosing sides, like in a chapter in *Animal Farm*.

As the Nicaraguan civil war was ready to break, my family

was also breaking up. My mother and sister had moved back to Paraguay, where they were born, because of the acrimonious divorce—our family's own civil war—and my younger brother and I went to Nicaragua to escape the tension of family turmoil. But this was a more urgent escape. My father ushered my fourteen-year-old brother and me, at sixteen, out of Nicaragua, though he remained to sort out what was left of the land of lakes, volcanoes, and poets. This was his home, and he wasn't going to be forced out. However, my home was now the United States.

With our family now spread across Central and South America, my brother and I didn't head back to our friends in Washington, DC, but instead went to stay with a family member in a rural part of the Midwest. It was American soil, but it was a very different United States from the one I had adjusted to and had learned to love.

Once again, I felt like I was crashing someone's party, someone who not only didn't invite me but wanted me thrown out. Having cut our American teeth in the nation's capital, my brother and I were suddenly in a small town. We were also trying to fit into a well-meaning household that wasn't necessarily in the market for two teenage refugees. The arrangement didn't work out, and we were soon on an adventure that took us from this friend's home to that friend's home, sometimes sleeping in an old car I had bought. I went from a sixteen-year-old adolescent gone astray to serving as the proxy parent of a fourteen-year-old who was as lost as I was, and not just in terms of geography.

Beaner, wetback, spic were barbed words I hadn't really heard growing up in Washington, DC, even during my rough start. Kids in DC made fun of me for being different and for my culture, but they weren't overtly bigoted. Now the epithets were flying at me like missiles in a video game, except I wasn't dodging them, but fighting them off as they made impact. I had always been La-tino, obviously, but didn't necessarily wear a big shiny L on my chest. Suddenly I was ready to put the Super Latino uniform on to fight my adversaries, including a gym teacher who would call me a wetback in front of the entire class. Something was different when an actual authority figure attacked me. The laughter from the other students was suddenly uncomfortable, and a corner was turned in terms of our acceptance.

Friendships were eventually forged with the supportive class-mates who appreciated our differences and our similarities. Even the most vocal abusers got past our being Latino, urban, and awk-ward. Thinking that I was finally able to fit in, I asked a beautiful, caring young lady to one of the dances, and she said yes. I drove to pick her up in the ill-fitting suit that I had borrowed from a friend. When I saw her at the door, she whispered a request to go along with telling her parents that I was Italian. "I think you can get away with it" were her comforting words to me. That L on my chest started pulsing and my feet beat a path to my 1974 Gran Torino as I felt the burn move from my torso to my face.

After coming back from the verge of combusting, I steered the car toward a park where some of the kids from school went to hang out. On the night of the big dance, this was a gathering place mostly for the unattached crowd. I noticed a girl I had a couple of classes with but had never really talked to. She seemed different. She was curious about where I was from, riddling me with questions about DC, Nicaragua, family issues, and how I'd learned to play the guitar. When she smiled at me, I felt a charge go through me like a car being jump-started. Within a week we were a couple, and I soon learned where she had gotten her em-pathy and acceptance from—her parents. After hearing about our situation, her parents invited my brother and me to live with them as part of their family. We felt special for the first time in a long time, thanks to the fostering family who wrapped itself around us like a warm comforter to weather a Midwest winter.

As I was bidding goodbye to my sweet-and-sour high school years and thinking of going back to the DC area to fulfill my childhood dream of attending the University of Maryland, I met with a guidance counselor. He greeted my aspirations with a smirk and then an *Oh, you're serious* look, followed by an admonishment that college was an unrealistic goal for me. When I graduated from the University of Maryland a few years later, I tracked down this guidance counselor to send him an announcement.

Now, decades later, I have my own family, a career serving the needs of the Latino community on a national level, and the American dream of a home in an idyllic setting for my children to grow up in. Not long after moving in, I was pulling weeds in my front yard when two of our brand-new neighbors stopped in front of my house. I smiled broadly, waved hello, then wiped the sweat from my brow and approached the older couple, who were waving me over enthusiastically. As I went to meet my new neighbors, the woman cupped her hands around her mouth and shouted, "Do you speak English?" I wrinkled my now-dry forehead and replied in a curious tone, "Excuse me?" She shouted back, at a volume and with an overenunciated cadence that was intended to break through any language barrier, "How much do you charge?"

 José Antonio Tijerino is the president of the Hispanic Heritage Foundation.

BROWN BOY, WHITE SUBURBIA

By Pej Vahdat

I grew up in a very white suburb of San Jose, California, called Almaden, where I was one of a handful of Iranian Americans in my neighborhood. I was in an even smaller minority of practicing Muslim kids.

I had a pretty great childhood. I played baseball and basketball until becoming a professional tennis player became my life plan. I had tons of friends, from the nerds to the cool kids. I was accepted and pretty much a normal kid doing normal things. But I always had this underlying feeling that I was an outsider. I was always either the only or maybe the only other brown kid in the group. I'll never forget how I felt around girls: like there was no way one would want a brown boyfriend. My close friend group was made up of all white kids, with the exception of one Indian and one African American kid. The subject of race was never really that prevalent, but it would pop up in jokes here and there. "Don't your parents work at 7-Eleven?" "Where's your magic carpet, Aladdin?" I tried to take them lightly, but there was one kid who always took it too far. He told me that since I was Muslim and not Christian, I was going to hell. He called me *muzzy*, a derogatory term for a Muslim. He thought that was funny, I guess.

The insults bothered me, of course, but at the same time I knew my culture was beautiful and different. And that gave me a sense of strength and confidence to combat the hate. That would serve me in my life. I definitely had moments of "whitewashing" myself, whether through the clothes I wore or by trying to bleach my black hair to look more like my friends'. But thank God I had strong parents who instilled in me a desire to own my heritage and where I came from.

I always had a passion for film, television, and theater. I spent hours watching movies and TV shows, getting lost in the stories. I watched school plays, in awe of how the other students could put themselves out there for a roomful of people. Secretly, I wanted to be able to do that, too. But I knew that was a pipe dream, because there was never anyone who looked like me onstage or onscreen. No brown boy could possibly be a successful actor. I never saw one anywhere, unless he was trying to kill Arnold Schwarzenegger or something. But the desire to get lost in a character, to be someone other than myself, was so appealing to me. And to have people get lost in a story that I was a part of was something I wanted so badly. I did some small roles in school plays in high school, a few lines here and there, but I always just reverted back to my crutch: sports.

Sports always gave me a sense of belonging. It was my way in, so to speak. My athleticism allowed me to feel like I was just like everyone else. And there was some validity to that. Sports was the reason I could hang out with cool kids as well as nerds. It was the one place that my race didn't matter. On some level, that's probably why I love sports so much to this day.

But it became harder for me to ignore my desire to act. As I got older, I thought I could be the guy who shows the world that Iranians and Muslims are just like everyone else. I could be the one to normalize my culture in America. I realize that in some ways this sounds pompous, but it was a calling I held in my heart and still do.

I put all the energy that I had put into sports into acting, but now I had a real passion for it, too. I was twenty-two years old, fresh out of college, and I moved straight to Los Angeles. I worked tirelessly to get an agent. At times I had to be my own agent, because legitimate agents always turned me down, saying, "We don't know what we can do with you." Auditions were few and far between, and when I did get them, 99 percent of the time it was for the part of a terrorist, a doctor, or a store clerk, all with only a few meaningless lines. But I would do almost anything just to get my foot in the door. I had to play the terrorist only once or twice, but I still look back and cringe.

Eventually my persistence paid off, and I got my break on a TV series for Fox called *Bones.* I was twenty-seven and had been fighting tooth and nail for five years for this opportunity: to play a character that—thanks to Hart Hanson, the show's creator, and Stephen Nathan, the executive producer—started fulfilling my dream of normalizing my culture. They wrote my character to show the world that Muslims aren't terrorists, that Iranians have a beautiful culture, and that brown men can be love interests.

My beliefs that my culture is worthy and that I have something to give because of my heritage have carried me to where I am today. I'm so unbelievably proud to be brown in America, and I wouldn't change it for anything. To this day, I have fans tell me they had no idea that Muslims could be normal Americans, or that Farsi is such a beautiful language. After my very first episode of *Bones,* I had a barrage of messages on social media from viewers saying that they hated my character, that he sounded like a terrorist. My character started off with an Iranian accent, but in a later episode it came out that he was faking the accent so people would treat him more kindly and not feel threatened by an American Muslim who happened to be a brilliant forensic anthropologist. The minute the accent was dropped, the messages changed: "I love him," "He's so good-looking," "Can't wait for his next episode."

The older I get, the more being this brown man has become an exotic and sexy thing to be—the complete opposite of how it was when I grew up. Of course, there is still a battle to be fought. Change takes time. I take great pride in representing my family and my culture, and I strive to continue to educate people about what a beautiful culture it is.

 Pej Vahdat is an Iranian American actor who can be seen on television shows and in films, including Shameless, Bones, Sneaky Pete, *and* Roman J. Israel, Esq.

THE PRACTICE OF SELF-LOVE

By Wade Davis

I don't remember the moment I unconsciously started to despise myself, but I do remember the day I consciously instigated the endeavor of killing off a significant portion of who I was.

It was my sophomore year in high school. I had transferred from a predominately black school to a larger, all-white school. I really never cared about much—everything was just noise. Not the type of noise you intentionally ignore, but the noise that's easy to forget, like the sound you hear when flying in an airplane. You hear it, but you can easily distract yourself and focus on something else. Anything else.

My something else was football.

Though I loved the game, it was also my hiding place. A space where I could exercise the anger building inside me from the internal hatred I was wrestling with.

During my sophomore year, when I realized I was attracted to boys, football provided me both with an outlet for my anger and with ecstasy. Football afforded me a place to exercise some level of control and dominance over others without accountability, because football *is* control and dominance. Yet I still felt too paralyzed to ever attempt to portray anything resembling authenticity, because I didn't believe my authentic self would ever be valued and affirmed.

The game of football doesn't reward weakness or vulnerability. Those qualities are acceptable only on the rare occasion when a coach or other leader expressly allows them, usually after a big victory, a massive defeat, or a tragedy.

My secret of being attracted to boys wouldn't be classified as an acceptable tragedy. Telling any of my teammates that I was gay would only compromise the tacit agreement that football is a space for "real" men. And that's the paradox of football. Sports gave me so much: family, brotherhood, and resilience. Yet the unspoken rules forced me to actively destroy any sensitivity, vulnerability, or longing for male intimacy.

When I fell in love with football, my love of the game was pure. I was just a skinny kid who understood the game intuitively and wanted to play hard and be with friends. And then I got older, and societal norms of power and control sank in; the conflict between femininity and masculinity (patriarchy) took the purity from my game, from my adolescence, and I began to separate myself from my reasons for playing sports to begin with.

As an incoming sophomore to my new, predominately white high school, I was already nervous and insecure, but I knew the script to follow because all the adults in my life had laid it out for me. Go to church and learn who controls you. Go to school and be taught why you need to be controlled. And then go home and perform the act of being controlled.

And never ask questions.

Never.

Questions were just the thoughts that were already answered while you weren't listening in church, in school, or when the grown folks were talking.

I was never taught the value of critical thinking or the power of curiosity to help me decide for myself what felt right. And because I never asked questions, I let others make sense of the world for me.

My sense of the world was rocked while I was sitting in class during my sophomore year. As all the students were walking into the room, I was already in my seat. And then he walked in. I don't remember his name, but I remember thinking, *He's cute. . . .*

Immediately panic consumed my body, as if everyone else in the room could hear my thoughts. I looked around to see if anyone else had noticed, but I soon realized my thought was mine and mine alone.

And I felt alone. More alone than at any other time in my life, because I knew what I felt was criminal.

Those around me had defined homosexuality not just as a sin, but as an act of self-erasure. Acting on my attraction to men would move me from a world where God's grace and my family's grace were my life preservers to a world where I would be surrounded by darkness on all sides. So my attempt to destroy those feelings inside me felt like an act of self-love. Not only did I attempt to destroy the feeling of male-to-male attraction inside me, I attempted to destroy anyone who reminded me of those feelings.

I remember the first time I saw John Smith at school. John was gay—but not just gay. John was GAY, in all caps. He wasn't able to hide the fact that he was gay, because he didn't perform maleness like other boys did. I believed that John didn't get the manhood script from his dad or his uncles.

I thought about John a lot. I imagined that there were no older men around him to explain to him the narrow rules of being a man. He didn't know that being hard, violent, and angry were the only acceptable modes of living for men. But I suspect John wanted to be free. And his expression of freedom meant he was in control, but it also resulted in other boys', including my, insecurity, and attempts to destroy him.

John was a friend of one of my close friends, and in private I was cautiously nice to him and studied him with great interest. He was my unicorn: something I wanted to touch, hoping to learn that he was as miserable as those in control had told me he would be.

Though I was never quite sure.

In public spaces I never initiated conversations with John. Talking to John would signal to others that I believed his sexual orientation was somehow normal, and anything that resembled a friendship would either signal that I was colluding with him to prove its normality or provide confirmation that I, too, was gay. So I attempted to create as much distance between John and myself as possible by bullying him.

My high school cafeteria was a site of trauma and violence for many of my classmates. My friends and I would congregate near the entrance and aim pejoratives at anyone who didn't have the social capital that commanded respect or the wit to offer a response that forced someone in my crew to cower in silence. John didn't enter the cafeteria often, but when he did, I would hurl a taunt in his direction in an attempt to confirm my complete disapproval of his lifestyle and signal to my friends that I, too, thought that being gay was abhorrent.

I knew I was different. But I accepted the fact that I would neglect my own humanity and annihilate myself in the process, ensuring that I would never discover freedom.

In my silence, I wanted to be John. I coveted his freedom.

I secretly yearned to have the ability to ask the questions John ordered the world to grapple with; I imagined John rummaging through the world, seeking out others who were asking the same questions.

Living in a world that never affirmed my existence smothered me in ways I wouldn't recognize until I was much older. I didn't know how to love myself. Although I was often told I *should* love myself, no one ever showed me how.

After my NFL playing days were over, I made a personal commitment to surround myself with those who made me feel *loved*. And I asked them these questions: What was their secret to self-love? Did they have a practice? Did they read about love? I wanted to be around people who actively interrogated and talked openly about love. Love toward self was my goal. And I knew self-love was an action. Not just an idea.

I realized I needed a practice of self-love. A daily, even hourly, practice of self-love that would repair my mind so I could fundamentally believe that I was *enough*. I hadn't hated John. I'd hated what he represented—a glimpse of what freedom could look like. Freedom I didn't have. And in my world, freedom equaled fear. John had exhibited the freedom to be himself without concern for the gaze of the world.

My public treatment of John was actually internalized hatred that I'd directed at him for doing something that I envied. He was practicing self-love by attempting to be his authentic self. John smiled at boys. John didn't emulate the stereotypical brand of faux machismo that my friends and I offered when talking about girls and sex. He walked around with his head high and didn't comport or contort walk and talk to make anyone comfortable beyond himself. John conveyed authenticity while the rest of us adhered to conventionality. And we despised him for that.

I imagine someone taught John a practice of self-love. I'm developing my practice, which gives me the capacity to give love to others freely and without recompense. And though I love myself more today than I did yesterday, my journey toward self-love starts anew every day.

 Wade Davis is a former NFL player who is currently a thought leader, a writer, a public speaker, and an educator on gender, race, and orientation equality.

GUTS

By J. W. Cortés

I didn't have to don a military uniform.

I didn't have to don a military uniform and travel over eight thousand miles to see and feel the rage, loss, and destruction of Vietnam. The New York Police Department had renamed the block that I was born and grew up on Little Vietnam. It was a creative attempt at describing the level of violence, drug abuse, and gang activity that had come to consume much, if not all, of the concrete, the brick, and the inhabitants of this neatly designed piece of urban dwelling in New York City.

It was 1993, and I knew deep in my troubled bones that things would continue to deteriorate. Wise corner men advised me— warned me, really—that there was so much more to life than "just this place," and that if there was ever an opportunity to get out, I'd better take it. But that place, despite its tumultuousness, did offer a strong sense of a proud, hard-knocks family heritage. Those were the pieces of the social fabric that I held on to.

I felt, just as so many other thousands like me felt and continue to feel, that one of the fastest, most assured ways of freeing my-self from the grips of an environment like Little Vietnam was to raise my right hand and essentially sign a blank check to the citizens of the United States of America for services rendered, payable up to the amount of my life. I needed a job, America was hiring, the ink and paper were ready, and so I took the opportunity and escaped Little Vietnam.

A few weeks later I found myself enlisting in the United States Marine Corps, a more acceptable form of punishment and torture than what I was used to, because it would be worth something more than whatever my previous combat tour that passed for a childhood could produce.

Don't get me wrong. I love America and the promise of what it represents, despite its imperfections. But it is somewhat ironic to me that a decade after I signed up to leave the hometown horrors of Little Vietnam, I found myself in a real combat zone, participating in the invasion of Iraq alongside so many others who had signed the same check I had. We were being told it was time to make good.

I'm often asked why I made the decision to enlist, what was the biggest motivating factor. For me the answer has always been twofold. First, my parents really tried their best to keep my brothers and sister and me out of trouble, and they instilled in us the importance of being leaders in our own right. The military seemed like a direct opportunity to do so. Second, I knew deep down that there was somewhere bigger, something more expansive, waiting out there for me. I needed to take the first steps toward that place, and I accepted that it would require a monumental risk on my part. I think back on how scared I was about heading to Parris Island, South Carolina, for military training, despite the fact that I had already been to places much scarier in theory. Like Rikers

Island, the jail I visited to see relatives, friends, and my biggest influence—my older brother. He was very much a leader in his own right, as head of one of New York City's most notorious gangs, the Latin Kings.

Despite the many challenges I'd faced, the theme constantly playing in my mind was, *I want to do better, become better, and feel better.*

What it takes to get out of a really bad place, physically, mentally, and spiritually, is listening to your heart when all the outside voices have been muted. It is believing in the daydreams that lift away into a life that could be and will be. It is nurturing and loving the one person you rarely spend quality time with and who needs you most: yourself.

My two sons will face tough times of their own, but I know that they must experience them. I know this regardless of what my overprotective-dad instincts tell me to do. Exams, interviews, and airplane turbulence are all fears better experienced than talked about. They lead to the really good stuff, the things that we can take back to our alone time, and that help us appreciate the smoother flying.

Little Vietnam, concrete jungles, and exploding Hollywood sets are reminders that in all of those places, I had guts—strong, blood-filled, oxygen-enriched guts. The same guts that are inside you. Trust that they are ready to accompany you, that they're dedicated to the owner who breathes life into them, and they'll make it that much easier to follow your heart.

 J. W. Cortés is a marine combat veteran, a singer, a philanthropist, and an award-winning actor currently playing Detective Carlos Alvarez on the TV series Gotham.

BLACK ANCESTRY AND ARTISTRY WIELDED AGAINST THE POLICE STATE

By Patrisse Khan-Cullors

My grandmother Jennie Johnson Simpson Endsley was the embodiment of *Southern Black girl magic*. She was born in 1912 in Baton Rouge, Louisiana, and after she turned two, her family moved to Texarkana, Arkansas. They finally settled in Oklahoma, where Grandma Jennie studied through high school.

Her mother, my great-grandmother, raised ten children and took care of their home, and her father worked as a laborer. Grandma Jennie lived on rural lands, rode horseback, and sang literally until the cows came home, herding farm animals at daybreak.

Not unlike other Black families, my great-grandparents moved throughout the US South, evading the Ku Klux Klan's terrorism. The KKK regularly harassed our family, and Grandma Jennie witnessed the characteristic violence of the Jim Crow era.

One of her close friends finally convinced her to move to Southern California, whereupon she became part of the twentieth century's diaspora of Black folks from the US South to the

West Coast. In Los Angeles, Grandma Jennie worked as a math teacher. She was also a singer. In the 1940s, she sang at Culver City's famous Cotton Club, carrying the poise and power of Black women's experiences in her song. Her life captured story lines that I've only read about in Octavia Butler's Afrofuturist novels.

Grandma Jennie planted the first seeds of performance art and its capacity for organizing in me as a child. She was one of my primary caregivers, as my mother worked constantly to provide a life with dignity for our family.

Her songs and stories were remarkably full of the wisdom of our roots: African, Choctaw, and Blackfoot. She shared with my siblings and me countless traditions, like those of my great-grandfather, a medicine man.

These histories were interwoven in my DNA and called upon me at an early age to refine my craft as an artist, a healer, and an organizer. Through my grandmother, I've transcended time and space, using similar artistry to fight the police state and its detrimental impacts on Black people, our families, and our communities.

I grew up in Van Nuys, in the San Fernando Valley. While adjacent to wealthier areas of Los Angeles, Van Nuys is predominantly working-class Black and Latino. Parks, recreational centers, and other resources were severely lacking in my community; liquor stores, homelessness, and police cars proliferated on the corners.

Historically, the Tongva, Tataviam, and Chumash lived on these lands as the first native peoples; however, once the Spanish arrived in 1769, their occupation resulted in the displacement and genocide of indigenous populations across California and the greater West.

I was a Black girl on stolen native lands. This history of geno-cidal warfare continued as the state waged the war on drugs and the war on gangs throughout our community.

This led to raging police terrorism. I constantly witnessed po-lice handcuffing Black and Brown boys and men along tagged-up walls and slamming them against cop cars. Most of the Black men in my community and my family spent time in juvenile centers, jails, and prisons.

Helicopter policing unleashed strong beams of light nightly, like UFOs in the sky, except we knew exactly where the lights came from and who they served—and, in our case, didn't serve. At a very young age, I realized I was in a police state.

My art became my release and my resistance.

For years, Grandma Jennie was the only audience for my per-formances. As a child, I was a runway model in our living room. Grandma Jennie always said she'd enroll me in dance classes. While she never had the opportunity to do so, she planted a deep seed in me that took root and continued to grow over time, blos-soming into the work I create today.

Growing up, my siblings and I traveled with Grandma Jennie to attend her performances with a Pacoima-based choir of over one hundred Black women. It was beautiful to see Black elders belting out the finest in soul, gospel, and contemporary tunes.

Before every performance, she led her choir in a collective prayer, followed by their rendition of "Amazing Grace." I con-tinue this ritual rooted in affirming our collective spirit before every one of my performances, albeit with chants and other af-firmations.

I attended Millikan Middle School's performing arts program, where, at eleven years old, I finally enrolled in dance. While I had danced in my apartment with my friends and my family, I hadn't been introduced to dance as an art form or studied it before.

Ms. Bailiff was the program director and dance teacher. I took her class at the end of the school day. After warm-ups, Ms. Bailiff would instruct us to dance across the floor, most days to Seal's "Kiss from a Rose." Seal became the unexpected official soundtrack to my early dance career.

In this process, I became familiar and comfortable with my movements. Unbeknownst to my classmates, my body released messages full of grief from the challenging times that my family faced.

My mother worked tirelessly to provide for us as a single mom and still we lived in poverty.

My older brother, Monte, whom I loved and admired as my hero, was taken from me time and time again because of the policing in our neighborhood. The first time I remember clearly. He offered to accompany me to my friend's house, and as we left our apartment building, an officer approached us. He asked, "Are you Monte Cullors?" My brother responded affirmatively and was immediately arrested. We never knew why.

More than a decade later, in 2006, I choreographed a piece with my friend Kelly Archbold when my brother and my father were being sent to prison. My brother was fighting a life sentence, and my father received three and a half years.

We danced to Lauryn Hill's cover of Sam Cooke's "A Change Is Gonna Come," an anthem of the civil rights movement. We dedicated the piece to people impacted by mass incarceration: our loved ones behind those dreadful concrete walls and steel bars, as well as our families outside. We burned sage, built an altar onstage, and used our bodies to convey the fear, separation, and heartache we felt. At the same time, we performed to break our imaginations free.

This piece arose from my family's artistic tradition that seeks to transform our trauma into healing. In hindsight, what dance and art provided for me is what they have for countless other Black people, from Nina Simone to Alvin Ailey to Chance the Rapper: a channel to talk about the Black experience.

As I learned of abolition in my early twenties, it became clear to me that my purpose was to weave art and organizing—despite people's attempts to dissuade me from this, since they considered these two areas of work worlds apart.

In today's repressive climate, with Donald Trump and Jeff Sessions at the helm of this country's government, we need more voices from our movement to tell our stories, past and present, and to imagine our futures.

My grandmother's legacy, my dance classes, and my growing artistic development as a young adult gave me a point of entry to build resiliency against the trauma that was entrenched in my community. My art form does not separate me from my reality; rather, it inspires me and strengthens my connection to the movement for abolition and liberation.

 Patrisse Khan-Cullors is an artist, an organizer, a freedom fighter, and a cofounder of Black Lives Matter.

I AM NOT SUSANNE—
I AM SOULAIMA

By Soulaima Gourani

I do a lot of networking. I talk to many new people every week as part of my job as an international trade adviser and lecturer.

Most people mumble their own names and forget other people's names easily.

To me, names are a very valuable part of my conversations. Names almost always carry stories. Stories about the people I speak to. They should *always* be something we care about.

Why do I have this thing with names?

In December 1975, I opened my eyes for the very first time, in the dusty North African country of Morocco, far away from Denmark. I was born into a Danish-Moroccan family, and I was different from birth—a little light brown outsider with curly hair among the Danish children my mother had from a previous marriage. The warmth of Morocco was replaced by the cold of Denmark, in northern Europe, in the first year of my life, but I did not become a Danish citizen until I was four years old.

Denmark refused to give me my citizenship despite the fact

that my mom is Danish. I could not be baptized when I was little because no priest would accept my name, Soulaima. The priests told my parents to change it to something normal and more Danish—it could be Susanne! They said I would have an easier life if they chose a common Danish name.

My parents refused. Of course.

It took my parents twelve years to find a priest who was willing to baptize me. I was now almost a teenager, and I was finally being baptized. My name was written into the church books as the first and only Soulaima, ever. But the mental scars were still there. I didn't feel accepted or included. Even today, when I have been given all the rewards I could ever imagine, I feel like an outsider sometimes. Nothing can wash away the shame of being a second-class citizen.

The priests were right. My life was not easy. But it was not just because of my name. It was because we were a family with mixed backgrounds—my Danish mom and my Moroccan dad. He came to Denmark with a lot of expectations and dreams. But people looked down on us. And when people look down on you, you do not get a lot of support from your community. What could have been a happy life became a struggle. Finding local jobs. Paying bills.

My Moroccan father did not exactly fit in in the Danish towns, with his dark skin, his different body language, food preferences, and music, even his exotic smell—not to mention his impulsive and straightforward personality. People talked about us. We were so different. Were we Muslims? As if that would be a disaster.

The Danes claimed they could not pronounce his real name, so he allowed them to call him Peter. He hated it. For most of his thirty-three years in Denmark, he never heard anyone using his real name. He decided to leave his religion behind to make our lives easier in Denmark. He tried his best to become Danish. But people never accepted him. It was humiliating to witness how hard he tried to get their blessing. I never wanted to be like that.

Danish families expected their children to marry other Danes. And if they did marry foreigners, then they would preferably be of the "better" kind: French, Spanish, German. But never a Muslim, or someone who really stuck out from the crowd. My grandmother never forgave my mom after she married my dad. All I wanted was to be "normal" and white.

My first fifteen years were miserable. My childhood was touched by death, financial hardship, abuse, and many moves. My dad could not keep a job for long, so we had to move from town to town.

Since we moved all the time, I was always the new girl in school. It was hard to start over and over—again and again. I hated most of the schools I attended. I never had a lunch bag. I was always hungry and dirty. Kids boycotted my birthday parties and parents forbade playdates with me.

I found it very difficult to focus on school, and I had a hard time managing my emotions. I had many conflicts with teachers and other students. I was always sad, angry, and a bit aggressive. Deep down, I am not like that. But I felt so unwanted because my home was such chaos, and it became my shield. I could not invite friends over. My parents became alcoholic, and I was ashamed of them. I became a tough cookie. I met the world on my own terms. Everyone has a breaking point—I was lucky this was not mine.

For as long as I can remember, I've wanted to stand on my own two feet, earn my own money (lots of it), and not depend on anyone. My first real ambition was simple: move away from home. I was sure I could do a better job taking care of myself than my parents could. My brother moved out of the house when he was sixteen, and my sister was in an institution. So it was only me left at my parents' house. I was twelve.

Seeing my brother gain his freedom ignited my desire. After a tough fight with my dad one night, I decided that I would leave the next morning. Pretend I was going to school. I packed some stuff and some money. I left behind a letter to tell them to leave me alone. I was very nervous and shaky that morning. I took the train to an island three hours from my home, where I had some extended family. I found my way to them and told them my story. They kept me until I was found by the police a few weeks later. I was nervous before they found me; I saw myself on the front of newspapers, and there was a search for me on TV and radio. I had never known of anyone running away from home. I am actually impressed that I knew how to do it.

When the police found me, I was sent to a children's institution. Months later I was put in foster care, and later still I moved into another youth institution.

I never moved back in with my parents. They offered to give it another try. But I did not want to.

My school kicked me out in seventh grade. It did not want me there once I no longer lived with my parents. Friends were no longer allowed to spend time with me—I could inspire them to run away, too, parents argued. So my teacher just left me standing alone in the schoolyard. Out of school. I could not grasp it. I was young, but I knew education was crucial. It took more than a year to find another school that would enroll me. It was a boarding school. Not one with a good reputation. But it took me, and I was happy to be back at school.

I knew all I could do was work extra hard to create a new and better future. I knew I would have to find a way to recover and to turn my pain into passion. I knew I was never going to be the most beautiful or the cleverest. I knew I was mediocre in many ways. But I was outspoken, and I did not put up with anything. These "skills" would one day take me far.

At seventeen, I worked both mornings and nights. As other students went out to party, I would go to work. And as I left work and others went home to sleep, I would go to my other job. I had many setbacks. But I found I had a very strong resilience—it could not make my problems go away, but it gave me the ability to see past them, find enjoyment in life, and better handle stress, broken hearts, anxiety, money issues, and loneliness.

I dedicated my own life to improving the lives of others. My seventeen ambassadorships with UN Women and Global Dignity, among many others, give me a platform to motivate and inspire thousands of young people. At Global Dignity, we believe dignity is an inherent part of the human condition. We believe most young people struggle with the question "Who am I?" and search for who they want to be. Our goal is to have an ongoing discussion with young people about values in a defining period of their lives. We believe that young people empower themselves with and through dignity.

I strive to make people brave, to allow them to shine, and I help them unleash their enormous potential and find their talents and passions. I want to create more Soulaimas in the world. Life is not about being perfect. Your career and personal life are all about having the courage and the ability to seize the opportunities you run into and the ones you create. There is no one formula. You will develop your own. Life will knock you down, so make sure you exercise your ability to come back stronger than ever. Soldier on!

Today I am happy living in the United States. Today I flourish. I really do. I am very aware of my happiness, because happiness has not been a constant factor in my life. And I proudly say loud and clear when people ask my name that I am Soulaima Gourani.

I am not a Susanne—I am a Soulaima.

And I am not half-Danish—I am double: Moroccan and Danish. I hope no one ever feels half-excluded. Let's make sure that you can say your name proudly and that there is no need to have a Western version of it. People should be able to learn to pronounce and to remember your name, and you should be proud of it, too.

What is your name? What is your story?

 Soulaima Gourani is a speaker, an author, and a special adviser to ministers, task forces, government think tanks, and private companies all over the world.

WE RISE

By Xiuhtezcatl Martinez

My whole life, I've been attending demonstrations and rallies and protests; I've had an awareness of the state of the planet. Environmental problems and the impact we as humans beings have on the world were always part of what I learned when I was growing up. This awareness was a superimportant part of my heritage on my dad's side—he is an indigenous Indian.

My dad is from Mexico City and is from the indigenous Meshika people. Our culture was illegal. Our ceremonies, our language, and our dances were outlawed in Mexico for many, many decades. Then there was a resurgence in the 1970s and '80s, when all of a sudden those ceremonies started to happen in public spaces. My grandfather reconnected to our ancestry and heritage then, passing them on to my dad, who passed them on to me. So I grew up with the songs and dances, with a connection to my ancestors, and that really shaped who I am. So much of who we are and what we do is a balance with nature—what we give to and receive from the world around us. That's the lens through which I see the world and my role in it, rather than feeling a sense of ownership. We belong to the planet. We have a responsibility to become part of it. Growing up with this knowledge helped me find my voice.

My mom is a badass. She got involved in climate change and environmental activism in Maui, Hawaii, in 1982. She started a school there called the Earth Guardian Community Resource Center. She had a vision of young people standing up and changing the world. She did a tour across the United States to carry that out, performing conscious hip-hop in twenty-nine states. My older siblings, my uncles, and my cousins were all part of that. And she met my dad on this tour. They became best friends, and then they fell in love.

When he was younger, my dad spent most of his time traveling and participating in different ceremonies and learning from different indigenous peoples. I follow my Meshika people's traditions, as well as Lakota traditions and ceremonies—the sacred dances of the Meshika, tepee ceremonies with the Lakota elders. There's a lot of fusion between the Meshika people and North American indigenous peoples. It is always about connecting to something greater than ourselves, to the energy of life all around us. That's what we pray for.

My dad was constantly exposing me to different ceremonial practices and different methods of spirituality. One of these was the prophecy of the eagle and the condor, which foresaw the union of the nations of North America (the eagle) and Central America (the condor). The Hopi people carry sacred water from New Mexico down to Mexico City, and the Meshika people bring the water back, and carry fire as well. This ceremony has been done twice; the second time, I participated, and we ran seven hundred miles to carry that water.

I was born in Boulder, Colorado, and grew up there, but I didn't go to school until third grade, so I spent my whole childhood just being a kid—experiencing life, learning academics from homeschooling, and taking every opportunity to do every kind of ceremony. Going to school was really interesting because Boulder is a very white community. Low-income housing programs allowed us to stay there, and it's a beautiful place to live. But we were always so different. I didn't really fit in with the white kids. My hair was long, my name was long. I was doing all these different things after school related to ceremonies and activism. Even though Spanish is my first language, I didn't really fit in with the Mexican kids either, because my name isn't Spanish and I look more indigenous. They would talk shit about me and I would understand them.

It was confusing for me trying to find a place—I feel that is most often the case with kids who are biracial. All the Mexican kids hung out together and lived in the trailer parks. All the rich white kids lived in the suburbs. And I didn't really fit in with either of those groups. A lot of my neighborhood was made up of Hispanic people living on low incomes, just like my family. I connected with people more easily outside of school, like playing soccer in the park.

The flip side of not fitting in was that I also learned to not really need to associate myself with one group, one race of people. Part of me wanted to fit in. But even as a young kid, when things were difficult socially, I would go home and sing songs or spend time outside or dance. The spiritual community I did these things with was where I found my place. And the activist community, too. Because no matter where we came from or what color our skin was, we were fighting for the same thing. We cared about something bigger than us. It was bigger than middle school or high school or wherever we were. It was about protecting our community. That brought us together.

Now that I'm dedicating more and more of my time to activism, and travel related to activism, it's hard to balance a normal teenage life at the same time. I've lost myself in that before. I've lost myself in what the world wants me to be versus who I am. Those are two different things. And I have gone through times in my life when I felt really disconnected and discouraged and questioned why I was doing what I was doing. But I've found the power of the opportunity that I have with my voice. And that's the balance, the fact that with the work I do comes a massive responsibility, and it's a really beautiful thing to be able to carry that. But I'm also growing up. I'm also learning what things are okay to say no to. Through song and music, I've found my way a lot. I've found a purpose. And now I'm traveling the world. I'm seeing places I would have never dreamed of as a kid.

My passion now is in the music and in the movement. I'm excited about being able to go from my place on the front lines to creating the action, the campaigns, the templates, and the platforms that are going to effect change in the world. I've been falling in with these really beautiful communities, especially the RYSE Youth Council. It's a project of Earth Guardians. It's twenty-six incredible young people from around the nation, leaders focusing on building and shaping the youth climate justice movements. And the 2018 election cycle is really important for us, too. There's a lot of things on the ballot that I'm really passionate about, like defending my home from fracking. There was a five-year moratorium on fracking that was just lifted, so they're going to start fracking wells all over eastern Boulder County. And that's really scary—that's getting closer to my family and a lot of people I love.

Facing adversity is the greatest opportunity we're ever given in life: to grow and to learn and to fight for how we want things to be as opposed to how they are. I've learned that regardless of what situation you're in or what kind of life you live, the greater the challenge, the greater the opportunity to rise. That's how I feel about our country right now. That's how I felt about battling my demons. I see each challenge as an opportunity to learn from our experiences and to understand where it is that we want to go. There's so much more light than darkness in the world. And if you don't see it, then you can create it.

 Xiuhtezcatl Martinez is a teenage indigenous climate activist, hip-hop artist, and powerful voice on the front lines of a global youth-led environmental movement.

REWRITING THE RULES

By Dr. Gail Schoettler

We weren't allowed to cuss, my twin sister and I, even though we lived on a cattle ranch and everybody knew real cowboys cussed. We wanted to be real cowboys, too, berating grumpy cows and balky calves with the brilliant curses we heard every day from the tough old men riding next to us.

Our younger brother could cuss because he was going to be a man. But girls had rules no boy had to follow, and using demure language was one of them. So my sister and I jumped on our ponies and rode across the hills, hurling curses at the squirrels and rabbits that scampered across our path, far from the ears of grown-ups determined to turn us into young ladies. That was my first attempt to break the rules that tied me down.

It was never spoken, but we knew boys could do anything they wanted and girls had to follow rules. Like sports—we could play sports in our PE classes, but not on our high school's teams. There were no sports for girls, except a ladylike version of tennis (none of Serena Williams's smashing serves). There were no soccer leagues for girls, no college teams, no women's professional sports. Our role was to watch and cheer on the boys as they won glory playing basketball, baseball, and football. We were on the sidelines and were sidelined in life, always the spectators, never the players.

Girls were not as important, born to be helpers rather than competitors, held back by all the rules imposed on them by their families and society. I was a tomboy because I wanted to do everything boys did. That was okay until I became a teenager and was expected to be a young lady. I didn't want to give up my tomboy freedom, but the pressure to do so was intense.

My beautiful, charming grandmother (who loved to be, and always was, surrounded by men) used to tell me that girls should never beat boys at sports or cards, that I wouldn't be popular or attract a man if I won. I wasn't good enough at the few sports allowed us, tennis and swimming (though not competitive swimming), to beat the boys, but I could and did trounce them on horseback. I could ride faster and do more tricks on a horse than any boy I knew. That gave me such a thrill that I decided there were times a girl ought to win, no matter the social consequences. And there were social consequences. My grandmother was right—boys in my high school didn't like girls like me who did something better than they did. When I was on my horse, I didn't care. When I got to school, I was miserable.

And then there was my mother, who one day pointed to a woman sitting under a hair dryer and getting a manicure in a beauty salon. "Look at that woman," she said. "She must have a wonderful personality, because she's not pretty, but she found a man who's willing to pay for her to get her hair and nails done." I couldn't help but wonder why she couldn't pay for those herself. My mom had a little money of her own because she took care of every calf in our area that was orphaned or abandoned by its mother—a difficult and all-consuming job—and she squirreled away some money when she sold those calves. But my dad paid for everything and made all the financial decisions. When I realized that, I decided I wanted to get a summer job—something in very short supply in a tiny ranching town. I think that day my mother told me I had to rely on a man for everything good in my life was when I began to long for my independence.

The unspoken societal rules about how to dress and how to compete extended beyond that, though. When I was in high school, girls were supposed to laugh off sexual "play" from boys if we wanted to be popular. No big deal if you were humiliated, you smiled and giggled. The big thing then was for a boy to grab a girl's crotch ("goosing," it was called). I felt violated and ashamed when it happened to me, but I tried to laugh it off so I wouldn't tick off the offending boy and so I'd be like the other girls. One time, though, the "goose" was particularly insulting. He actually stuck his finger into my crotch, which horrified and shamed me, and I slapped the boy in the face. I'd had enough. To my shock, he slapped me back—and I cried. But no boy ever goosed me again. I learned that standing up for your dignity is painful, but it feels so much better than giving it up.

I was on the B-list of girls after that, but I decided then that I cared less about being popular and more about being respected. Though I don't think I knew it at the time, that episode helped me respect myself and begin to move beyond the social rules girls were expected to follow without regard to their own needs.

Years later, after I graduated from college, Title IX began to open the world of sports and scholarships to girls. Colleges could no longer discriminate against women in granting scholarships or offering sports. Title IX taught me that there are ways to change the rules—both the government's rules and society's—and that you don't have to stand up for yourself all alone. It woke me up to politics and action, though ever so slowly.

I had no knowledge, however, of any woman who took on the restrictive rules that applied only to girls, whether in sports or a family or a workplace. During my college years, my friends and I never talked about careers. We weren't supposed to have careers. We were supposed to get married and have children and take care of our families. Our husbands would make the decisions for us, even though we secretly knew we could change the world if given the chance. Until we had children, we could be secretaries or nurses or elementary school teachers, but not doctors or electricians or miners. And once we had children, we would stay home and take care of them—until they left home, and then what would we do? We would have no money of our own, no job skills, no role to play in society.

Until the 1970s, girls could not get birth control unless they were married. Abortions weren't legal. It was unimaginable to have sex outside of marriage, but couples did have sex, of course, and if a girl got pregnant, it was her fault because she shouldn't have had sex in the first place—another rule for girls that didn't apply to boys. I watched some of my high school and college friends, still teenagers, reluctantly marry the fathers of their babies because they thought they had no other choice. Girls had to play by the rules; boys did not. Unwed mothers were shamed; unwed fathers were just being men. I wondered why the rules were so unfair, but I didn't know what to do about it.

I did see a few women in politics as I was growing up, mostly on school boards. I remember thinking that that must be something I, as a girl, could do. And maybe I could make the rules if I was elected to something. But I never saw a woman in state or national politics other than as the wife of the eminent politician, forever standing behind her man.

I didn't like that. I didn't really plan a career in politics, but I did take advantage of the opportunities that literally popped up in front of me. I was always afraid that I wasn't up to whatever elected position appeared in my path, but maybe because I had learned to take risks on my horse when I was a kid, or because I took the risk of standing up for myself in high school, I just plunged in and decided I could figure out how to do the job or win the election once I had launched myself. And I persuaded myself that if someone asked me to do something, maybe I had what it took to be successful. But I was always scared. I had to begin to trust myself in the face of all those who said a woman couldn't do it and just plow forward. Most of the time, it worked. I learned to believe in myself.

I was elected to the school board, then state treasurer and lieutenant governor of Colorado. When I ran for governor of Colorado, people told me a woman couldn't be governor, but I didn't believe them. I lost that election by just several thousand votes, but I still know in my heart that women can—and should—win. Afterward, my closest friend and I decided that women would win elections only when other women supported them. We created Electing Women, a group with the goal of electing women governors, senators, and president. We've started a dozen Electing Women chapters around the country to help women run and win so that no one will ever again be able to say, "A woman can't do it." When women win, we silence that statement once and for all.

 Dr. Gail Schoettler has been a US ambassador, Colorado's lieutenant governor and state treasurer, Douglas County's school board president, and a businesswoman.

BEYOND THE BASELINE

A Conversation with Jason and Jarron Collins

Jarron: I fell in love with basketball around the age of ten. It was just how so many people imagine that kind of thing happens: playing in upstate New York, in my grandparents' driveway, against my brother. I loved playing, shooting, scoring, defending, and, most of all, winning.

Jason: I fell in love with basketball the first time I dunked a basketball in a game—in the eighth grade!

Jarron: As a teenager, I just knew I was going to play in the NBA. I had all the confidence in the world. The doubt crept in in my senior year of college. I hadn't left school early, I wasn't ranked as highly as I thought I should have been, and subsequently I was drafted late in the second round. The odds of making an NBA team were not in my favor. It served as a reality check, and I had a challenge and a test put before me to see if I could actually achieve my dream. I worked harder to make it happen the summer after getting drafted than I had in my entire life.

Jason: I thought I might not make it to the pros after dealing with injuries in my first two years at Stanford University. I had two knee surgeries my freshman year and a wrist reconstruction surgery my sophomore year. Because of my wrist injury, I had to totally relearn how to shoot a basketball and change the form on my jump shot. To this day, I have limited range of motion in the wrist of my shooting hand.

Jarron: Our biggest obstacle as teenagers was one that we did not perceive as such. It was the sacrifice we had to make to achieve our dreams. We were not living the typical life of teenagers. We were not attending dances and hanging out on weekends. We were practicing on several different basketball teams after school, doing our homework late at night, and playing games on weekends.

We were raised in a household full of love. My family instilled confidence and passion and a sense of self-worth, and I knew who I was as a black person in America. My most vivid experience with racism came in the third grade; I was changing in the locker room and a white kid was yelling, "Look at the n——er and his black skin." In that moment, I felt angry, upset, and confused. Ready to fight. For me, it wasn't necessarily about staying positive, but more about recognizing the truth: that there are people in this world who live with hate in their hearts. I wasn't going to let their ignorance bring me down.

Jason: Growing up, I was always aware of my race. I went to schools that were predominantly white and felt subtle racism from some classmates. I've had to deal with a few instances of "driving while black," when police officers pulled me over for some highly questionable offenses. The first time I was confronted with blatant, in-your-face racism was when I was living in Atlanta. It's called a "welcome to the South" moment. I was on the golf course in one of the nicer parts of town, Buckhead. I was playing with three strangers, all white guys in their mid-twenties. One of them said the n-word out of the blue, clearly trying to provoke a negative response from me. I immediately walked off the golf course in shock.

Jarron: My biggest obstacle appeared when I was twenty-three years old and into my second year of living my dream as an NBA player. I suffered a catastrophic knee injury, tearing two ligaments and my meniscus—all of which you need in order to play basketball. The injury required surgery, and the road back to being able to play basketball was the most difficult I had ever faced. All of us face obstacles in life. Either you can be deterred or you can overcome. You choose. How hard do you want to work? Nobody cares it isn't fair.

Jason: I realized that I was gay in junior high school. It took me until my mid-thirties to finally accept it. I lived with a lot of fear, anger, denial, and pain for most of my life while fighting the truth. Fortunately, I had basketball as an outlet for those pent-up frustrations and feelings. I often played angry out there on the court, which turned out to be a good thing because it helps to be aggressive when you're playing sports. When I finally did come out, I was humbled by the outpouring of support that I received in response.

Jarron: Our parents have always made the sacrifices that allowed us to achieve our dreams. My family and grandparents were the driving force and all helped me achieve my dream to play in the NBA.

Jason: My biggest motivation to persist through adversity came from my family. My support system has always been my family members, and they've given me confidence and encouragement to overcome adversity and achieve my goals. My best advice to young people is to find that support system that encourages you and challenges you to dream big. I was fortunate to have family members who did that for me, but as I got older, I had friends from school who also did that. Surround yourself with positive people who will have your back through thick and thin. Try to eliminate negative people from your inner circle.

Jarron: Be strong. Be determined. Set your goals. Write them down. Understand the importance of being proactive. People want to help people who help themselves. Appreciate the skill of time management. There are only a certain number of hours in the day, so you want to maximize every moment. Sacrifice may be required to achieve your goals. My only word of caution for those living in this day and age is to recognize that your digital footprint is forever. Anything you say or do on the internet can have an impact on the way people view you and treat you.

Jason: First, be consistent with your behavior and your actions. Second, remember that your reputation will go places that you will never go, so make sure that when you interact with people, you treat them the right way. Lastly, you can judge a lot about

people by the company they keep, so keep good people
around you.

 Jarron Collins is a former NBA player who spoke with his twin brother, Jason, at the Democratic National Convention in 2016.

 Jason Collins is a former NBA player and was the first male active player in any of the four major American professional sports leagues to announce that he is gay.

MY GROWTH THROUGH DROUGHT

By Kiara Nirghin

Inspiration. The ability to spur a revolutionary change in the world, a springboard to an idea that can impact thousands of human lives, the single thought that gave you the affirmation to follow your eccentric idea—it all starts with one word: *inspiration*.

I have been asked countless times what exactly inspired this young, female South African to take on the drought. The real answer is: there is no answer. There should never be one answer that can be compressed into a few winged words. My inspiration is too complex to fit into a simple sound bite like "Well, I personally experienced the drought."

My name is Kiara Nirghin. I am eighteen years old, I am from South Africa, and I am a girl. Even when ignoring my gender and the lack of focus on scientific innovation in my country, not everyone believes that a teenager could come up with an invention that could stop a worldwide epidemic. I entered the Google Science Fair in 2016 and won its Community Impact Award for the Middle East and Africa and eventually the overall fair. A few weeks later,

Time magazine named me one of the 30 Most Influential Teens of 2016, and what can I say? My whole life changed.

I vividly remember, at the age of six, staring at the white paint that marked the lanes on the school's grass. I was wincing, slightly unsure of myself, while my knee grazed the starting line of the hundred-meter lane. The siren sounded. I gave it my all, my knees burning, my chest thumping, and my eyes closed in concentration. I finished in sixth position. Which might seem satisfactory, if the race had not consisted of me and five other preschoolers. I wish I could say that I wore my sixth-place badge with pride, but after a bit of six-year-old introspection, I knew I could not.

I am the youngest in a family of five. Being the youngest of the three siblings meant that I could very often conduct what I like to call "primary research" on what to do to be better. I remember watching my sister in Grade 9 build an elaborate and intricate history project on the Battle of Stalingrad with suspended model aircraft. When my turn came to do the same project, I suspended the aircraft just a bit higher, made my project just a bit more detailed, and added a few—just a few—more soldiers. The competition between my sister and me taught me from a young age to see what had been done and how it could be better. This undoubtedly led to my love of improving upon other scientists' work.

As a ten-year-old, if I was interested in the thrust of an airplane or the combustion in a car's engine, I opened a book or website or posed the questions to my science teacher to douse my burning curiosity for the day. Looking at it now, I realize that every single scientist, or any influential person in the world, has to be curious. You can never grow complacent about what you know and what you do not. Drawing the line of your understanding both inside and outside the classroom and constantly seeking to push it back is what makes combating something like the global drought slightly less intimidating.

I soon realized that I possessed different interests from my friends. Those who discussed the latest film in their free time did not quite understand why I was always so invested in Bill Nye's science videos. It is not like I was discouraged from pursuing my love of science as a young girl; however, there were always a few concerned eyes as I devoured a newly befriended textbook.

At the age of thirteen, I was diagnosed with bilharzia, a parasite-induced disease, and three months later with bacterial meningitis. I was hospitalized for a portion of my Grade 8 year, and, being a diligent student, I howled when I realized I would not be taking the midyear examinations. I recall lying in my hospital bed with a piece of paper and a few colored pencils to create my entry in my school's stained glass competition. I learned that if I tilted my neck at a sixty-degree angle, the excruciating pain from my cervical vertebrae stopped for just long enough for me to color in a vine border.

After my recovery, having personally felt the impact that science can have on the world, I found that my love for science quadrupled. I started to research the construction of seemingly insignificant daily objects. I soon realized that understanding the mechanisms within a wristwatch was just not challenging enough for my curious mind. I began researching all sorts of major problems that my community and country were experiencing.

I was immensely interested in the major crisis of rhino poaching that the South African wilderness was enduring. After researching the crisis, I was motivated to search for just a while longer—this time for information and statistics not on rhino poaching but on the chemical nature of thermochromic dyes that I believed could be the answer to protecting these animals and eliminating the problems of the permanent dyes in use in the industry. Conservationists had already begun dyeing the horns of rhinos bright pink, rendering them useless to poachers. But this permanent discoloration also hurts the animals' ability to camouflage themselves in their surroundings, making it harder to hide from poachers and other predators. My solution was to develop a temperature-sensitive dye that becomes bright pink only once the animal has died and its body temperature changes. One stumbling block in the path to this scientific innovation is the sourcing of materials to test on, but watch this space! My curiosity will never cease to exist.

One thing led to the next, and soon I was researching the highly publicized issue of the drought that South Africa, along with 66 percent of the world, was experiencing. One of the major effects of the drought was the strain that it was putting on South Africa's crop supply, which meant that South Africa had to import most of its crops for the survival of many communities. After watching my cousin change her baby daughter's diaper, I was fascinated by how much liquid a simple diaper could absorb. I found out that the powder within the diaper was called a super-absorbent polymer, and it already had an extensive range of applications, one of them in the agricultural industry. These polymers were added to soil in order for it to retain large amounts of water relative to its weight. Through periods of drought, the polymers could support the growth of plants by acting as small reservoirs of water in the soil beneath them. However, the superabsorbent polymers available to the agricultural market were expensive, not biodegradable, and chemical-based, which ultimately limited their use. My goal was to emulate the properties of a chemical-based superabsorbent polymer but make it low cost and environmentally friendly.

I started looking at the molecular structures, chemical compositions, and polymer chains of these traditional superabsorbent polymers. Research in academic journals and my love for baking led to the realization that these characteristics can be found naturally in orange peels, which (I discovered after months of rigorous experimentation in my garage and kitchen) through emulsion polymerization with the oils in avocado skins can create a polymer that retains more water, keeps soil moister, and assists the growth of taller plants than commercial superabsorbent polymers do. I was lucky enough to be given an international platform to take my invention to new heights and continue with research and development. With the use of my invention, food security in agricultural drought disaster areas could increase by 73 percent, and rest assured, it will. With the assistance of more capital funding from agricultural corporations for further research and development, the invention's intended results will soon be achieved.

So one could say my inspiration was a dirty diaper! But after the last consolidation of my results, I realized that getting to that moment, with an invention in my hands that has the potential to impact thousands of lives, would not have been possible without my mum, my dad, my sister, my brother, and my fellow scientists who assisted in the research of the project, or without the disappointing school race, my illness, the decision to search just a bit longer, and all the other moments that encouraged me to believe that I can, as a young female scientist, make a difference.

 Kiara Nirghin won the Google Science Fair, and its Community Impact Award for the Middle East and Africa, with her invention No More Thirsty Crops.

L'AMOUR, MAYBE NOT

By Shruti Ganguly

You remember your first heartbreak—that acute pain your chest feels while your mind still tries to process the situation, when you think that your life is just over and that you can't possibly go on. . . . When you may lock yourself in the closet, with only enough ventilation coming through that when they find you, you'll still be breathing.

I was in middle school and totally in love with the boy next door. Roger, half-French and half-Lebanese, fair with flushed cheeks, thick glasses, and braces to curb his buckteeth. While I grew up with a grass-is-always-greener attitude, deeming things outside my own household to be better, Roger was quite the opposite. He even convinced me that I needed to get glasses and braces to be of worth. I cried and flailed my arms when the dentist claimed I had straight teeth and the optometrist said I had twenty-twenty vision. The curse continues and I am still braces-less and glasses-less today.

It was the time when TV shows like *The Bold and the Beautiful* and *Santa Barbara* hit the international satellite waves and made it to our households in Muscat, in the Middle East. Roger admitted he liked me, and he kissed my cheek one evening in my ground-floor dining room. My brown skin turned a shade of deep pink as the heat reached all the way down to my toes. I was floating. My dreams, night and day, carried me to some American suburb where Roger and I would find ourselves conversing in soap-opera-style dialogue: "No, Shruti, you must know that I'll leave everything to be with you." "But, Roger, how can you? When you are still with her?"

In my pubescent dreams, my female instinct was still present. Who was *her*?

. . .

It was Roger's younger sister Sarah's Holy Communion. Not everyone from the neighborhood was invited, and it was going to be mostly their friends from the French school. My brother and I went to the Indian school and had a different set of weekday friends. I wore my favorite top—it was navy-inspired, dark blue with white life buoys tangled in red rope.

After my mother dropped me off at the church, she left to meet my brother and father at some tennis academy. I didn't know anyone besides Roger. He sat in the front pew with all his friends, speaking only in French and laughing aloud. Roger saw me, but he seemed to avoid my gaze. With no one else to join, I chose to sit next to Louisa, their maid from India, who ushered me over to her as the ceremony was about to start. I sat alongside various women, mostly from South India, who worked as nannies and housekeepers for the French families who were sitting in front of us. They, too, conversed animatedly in their own language—Konkani, which I also couldn't understand—while rewrapping their brightly colored saris around their heads and shoulders. Along with my navy shirt, my heart started to sink. In the crowded church, I felt excruciatingly alone. There were no smartphones back then to distract me from the reality of the situation—it was the first time I felt displaced from my own culture or from my own social group, the first time I was the "other."

After the service, we were meant to be going to a reception at the Ruwi Novotel Hotel, which Roger's father managed, but there was some time to kill, so everyone gathered in the church playground. I took a deep breath and went over to say hi to Roger and his friends. A pretty blond girl, Alexandra, stood next to him. Upon seeing me, she uttered some garbled words, and they all turned around and raced each other to the other end of the playground, leaving me behind.

I returned to Louisa and her friends, who were pushing a merry-go-round, much to the enjoyment of the various French toddlers. I joined in, distracted and distressed, pushing the circle around. The kids shouted at us, *"Vite, vite"*—go faster. After a minute or so, I yelled back in response, sensing a sudden rush of deep pain. My right hand had gotten stuck between a concrete block and the speedily revolving ride. Blood started to emerge, and the children raced off to their parents, their screaming octaves higher than my own. I felt faint, and couldn't see past the ocean of saris as the women crowded around and tried to pry my hand out from the tight gap.

Roger's mother rushed over, horrified. I had lost some of the skin off several of my fingers, and they were bruised and bloody. I fought the tears to save face, hoping that maybe now Roger,

Alexandra, Pierre, and Charles would pay some attention to me, that sympathy would be on my side. A doctor friend came over, saying my hand would be fine and just needed some ice.

I was made to sit down, drink some terribly sweet juice, and then insert my throbbing hand into a batch of ice, protected by the floral paper napkins someone had grabbed from the church pantry. Five minutes went by and the socializing continued, while Louisa and her friends remained by my side. Roger decided to walk twenty feet over to see how I was doing. Maybe this unexpected pain and plan were working after all? I forced a smile and said it was no big deal. Roger then left as quickly as he had arrived, informing his mother that he would be going in Alexandra's car to the party.

I was ushered over to Roger's mother's Peugeot, and we headed toward the hotel, which also happened to be very close to my house. There I was met by our housekeeper, Selena, and my younger brother, Sumir. While Selena freaked out and cared for my hand, Roger and his friends were at the buffet, scooping out caviar onto their plates. He then came over and insisted I try some. It was unclear if he was doing this to make me feel better or to challenge me, as all his friends stared with mild enthusiasm. Fish roe was definitely not my thing, but turning it down would be deemed a cultural insult.

I held my breath and bit into a melba toast laden with some Russian varietal. It suddenly felt that the entire room had stopped talking, that they all turned toward me to observe, with a critical eye, this prolonged moment. The champagne ceased to bubble, the crudites lost their é, mouths shaped in the word *non* froze around me as if I were surrounded by goldfish.

After two extremely loud crunches—after which half the thin

toast broke into pieces and fell to the ground—the pungent, bitter taste finally assaulted my taste buds. I simply couldn't hide my disgust and spat out the rest into a napkin. Roger stared in shock, and in a corner somewhere a young girl whispered something to the shadows: "But, Roger, how can you?"

I don't remember much of the rest of the evening. Perhaps my memory past that point was clouded by detachment. Or perhaps it was shrouded in the intense pain of my breaking heart, a pain that stung deeper than that of my right hand. With every bruise, the skin eventually heals; that first heartache will not be the last. But that first realization of otherness—that's the one that stays the longest. I learned that, in this case, my non-Frenchness was obvious. Perhaps it had been clear to everyone but me. You don't ever realize you are the "other" until someone else makes you conscious of it.

When you then become aware of the color of your skin, the dark pigment of your eyes, the flick in your accent—that it's curry versus caviar, saffron versus rouge—that incident becomes definitive. Here I was, trying to impress the boy I fancied—adopting everything I could to be more unlike myself, more French perhaps. *C'est cool, non?* It took me only a bruised hand, a broken heart, and assaulted taste buds to come to terms with the fact that perhaps I was just different.

 Shruti Ganguly is an award-winning filmmaker based in New York City.

WRITING MY OWN STORY

By Jillian Mercado

Not so long ago, I realized that the story of my life was one that society had written for me. I had been handed a book about my life that I always read as true—and finally realized wasn't. I decided to write my own book, with my own pen and paper. To do the things that I wanted for myself and no one else. Until this moment, I had been told that the circumstances in my present life were punishing me for something that had happened in a past life, and that the only thing I could do about it was wait for a better life the next time around.

As a child, I was very shy and lived in a world full of imaginary people and places. My parents made sure to raise us all (I am the oldest of three girls) as equally as possible, so I never thought of myself as different—in a negative way, that is. I knew that I had to attend physical therapy, and that my parents and doctors were constantly on the lookout for any new medical advances that could possibly help with my muscular dystrophy, and that walking around the apartment was tougher for me than it was for my sisters, but even with all those differences, I still had a pretty "normal" childhood. As I got older and became more aware of my surroundings, though, I noticed people treating me differently than they treated my younger siblings. They spoke to me with more care, using a tone of voice they might with a baby—which especially bothered me since I was the oldest. I began to realize that, in this case, being different wasn't necessarily a good thing. I found these thoughts slowly seeping through my mind, brainwashing me into believing something about myself that wasn't true: that being different was more of a curse than a blessing.

There was one moment in middle school when I began to realize that this was not true—that I had been right before society's perspective of me erased my own. Our school was scheduled to go to an ice-skating rink. I was superexcited to go, because not only would I be able to hang out with my friends outside of school, but the last time I had visited an ice-skating rink had been several years before, and I had loved it. All the kids were packing up their schoolbags to head downstairs to the bus when I was called into the office to speak with the assistant principal. I wasn't sure what was going on, but I quickly made my way there. There were a few other kids also in the office, each with some sort of disability, and we were questioning one another, trying to find out why we were there. All I kept thinking was, *I hope this doesn't make me too late to sit with my best friend on the bus.* Minutes later, a teacher entered and told us with a great big smile, "We are going to the movie theater to watch *Fantasia 2000* in IMAX!" I asked the teacher about the ice-skating trip, and she responded, "Well, how are *you* supposed to ice-skate?" I was heartbroken. I should have said something, but I didn't. I could tell from the other kids' faces that they were confused, too, but trying to pretend that everything was fine.

Except for one girl. She refused to go to the movie theater and demanded to speak to the principal about this change. She spoke up about the injustice of the situation, questioning why we didn't have a say in this change of plans. Her body language was so powerful, commanding attention. I was inspired by her confidence and her willingness to fight for what was right. I took mental notes, and these notes began to negate all the things I had been believing about myself for years. What would happen if the rules were questioned? Where had these rules come from in the first place? Were we allowed to refuse this way of thinking? It was a powerful moment, but everything led back to the same disheartening answer: it is what it is.

Years later, when I was about seventeen years old, I woke up crying, desperate to figure out why my life had to be so tough. I wanted to feel like I had when I was a child: carefree, unaware that my differences would define me and hold me back. Moments like this began to happen more often—moments of frustration that eventually became moments of clarity that helped me realize that I wasn't going to let society write my own story for me.

Being a teenager with a disability wasn't easy. Not only did I have to go through the usual turbulent journey you experience as a teen, but I had a physical shadow following me every step of the way. I had a paraprofessional, someone assigned to assist me, and having a person at my side around the clock meant I never had the freedom to explore on my own. I was assigned a paraprofessional even before I had a sense of what that actually meant or entailed. It was never the same person, so every year from the age of three to the age of eighteen I had someone different looking out for me. Someone I had to retell my story to, what I felt comfortable with as far as helping, and things that I was able to do without any help at all. I was pretty independent, so the explanation of what I could do on my own took a while.

I don't blame my paraprofessionals, or my parents for assigning them, but rather the rules that led society to believe that people with disabilities cannot explore on their own. That we can't vocalize our own needs. There's an assumption that we need help during every moment of our lives. As a shy teenager, I was screaming from within to challenge this idea.

There were a lot of little moments when having a paraprofessional interfered with my life in a negative way. If I had a crush on a boy, my paraprofessional always seemed to know about it—and if he passed by, she would ask him to eat lunch with me or sit near me in class. I'm pretty sure it was with a good heart, but to me it was extremely embarrassing. My parents had to sign permission slips every day to let me eat lunch outside with my friends without my shadow. Even harder was making new friends. I had to make sure that they understood that I had someone with me at all times, so having secrets or girl time was to be done outside of school only.

When I finally found the power within to speak up, my life changed forever. I wasn't going to allow other people to write my life story. With respect to the rules, I decided that I would defy them. Once I allowed myself to be my most authentic self, I saw that I had more power than I ever thought.

I'm here to tell you that once you grasp your own life choices and know that you can handle any curveball life may throw at you, you have the power and strength to write your own story. You have the power to go on as many adventures as you want, despite anyone else's opinions.

I have lived my whole life in a wheelchair, never experiencing what it is to walk freely, but I am free. I am adventurous. I will continue to do whatever it is I love doing, despite whatever limitations or excuses that may come with having a disability. I see my disability as an added bonus to my life. It doesn't own me—in fact, it is something that I have become best friends with. Don't worry about the things that you can't change. Celebrate them! I promise you, your story is more fascinating than you think. So what will your next chapter be?

 Jillian Mercado is the most recognizable model with muscular dystrophy and has worked with multiple industry icons.

THE ACCIDENTAL ACTIVIST

By Gavin Grimm

Four years ago, I began my sophomore year of high school. I had come out to my family and friends as transgender the summer before. I also came out to the school administration. I told them that I was a boy and asked that my gender identity be respected. They told me that they would do what they could to ensure that teachers and administrators would call me Gavin and use male pronouns when referring to me. Additionally, they said that if anyone gave me any kind of trouble, it would be resolved right away. By the time school started, I had legally changed my name, and I was going to be starting testosterone within the year.

Despite the positive reception from the administrators, I was still anxious. My community is a fairly conservative one, and I wasn't sure that I'd be accepted for who I was. Because of this anxiety, I did not initially ask permission to use the boys' restrooms. I was not yet accustomed to advocating for myself. I was worried that I would be asking for too much, too soon, and that my peers' reactions would be negative and hostile. So instead I used the restroom in the nurse's office.

The nurse's office was far away from my classes that year. It took much too much time out of my day to use the restroom, especially when I was usually just down the hall from a perfectly functional boys' room. So I approached the administration a second time. This time, I asked to use the bathrooms that corresponded to my gender identity—that is, the boys' rooms. My peers' reactions had been mixed, but not aggressive, which had been my primary concern. People would either just go with it or talk behind my back. My principal told me the following day that I had his permission to use the boys' restrooms, and I did. For a period of roughly seven weeks, I went in and went out with no altercations. No physical or verbal confrontations occurred. No restroom misconduct by or against me. This seven-week period showed me what it was like to be supported and validated by my school, and it gave me confidence that I would be able to live out a normal school year, unencumbered by restroom politics.

Unfortunately, this was a false sense of security. After that seven-week period, the school board was going to hold a meeting at which a public conversation about my genitals and restroom usage would be had, and I was not notified first. My mother and I found out by chance less than twenty-four hours before the meeting was to happen. An old friend of my mother's had noticed a post going around Facebook. It was a rallying cry by adults in my community, urging people to show up to the meeting in order to "keep that girl out of the boys' room."

In November 2014, I went to the meeting and spoke at it. I thought it was important for me to represent myself when they were speaking about me. After all, no one else was going to. Family and a few good friends stood by me, but nothing could have prepared that insecure fifteen-year-old for what was to come. People speaking out against me made an obvious, grandiose point of referring to me with female honorifics and pronouns. They warned me that I was going to be raped or otherwise abused. They suggested that boys would sneak into the girls' bathrooms and harm their children. In reality, no one was concerned about my safety. They were afraid of confronting something that upset their narrow worldview. I was not in any danger. Those seven weeks, and at least two years of public men's rooms before that, proved it. The decision was ultimately postponed.

A month later, a second meeting was held. The rhetoric at this meeting was even more inflammatory. Word had spread throughout the community and people turned up in spades. After each frenzied remark, clapping and hollering tore through the room. People were cheering for the most ill-conceived, intellectually destitute, blindly emotional comments and arguments that I had ever heard. I was absolutely blown away by the lack of common decency in that room that night. The school board issued a statement about its policies that, in my view, was a clear attempt at keeping up appearances within the community. The members of the board wanted to silence critics and grant themselves the ability to appear as if they had been *so* accommodating and had just bent over backward, thus making me seem unreasonable. It read:

"It shall be the practice of the [Gloucester County Public Schools] to provide male and female restroom and locker room facilities in its schools, and the use of said facilities shall be limited to the corresponding biological genders, and students with gender identity issues shall be provided an alternative appropriate private facility."

I chose to fight that day. At the time, I did not know what that entailed. But it was not an option for me to give up and go quietly back into the prison of discrimination. I was not going to live out the rest of my high school years in segregation—at least not without doing everything I could to fight it. From that time on, I have been devoted to this fight. Despite hearing those remarks about me, I moved forward. Despite being exiled from the spaces my peers shared freely, I moved forward. Despite the conversation taking up years of my high school career, I moved forward. Not for myself, but for others. That is because this isn't about me. It isn't a conversation just about whether or not Gavin Grimm would be able to use the boys' restroom before he was out of high school. It is a conversation about perseverance of transgender youth all across the nation. Many of them—in fact, most of them—do not have the good fortune to go to an affirming school. Even fewer have the platform to fight back. Ideally, this would be a conversation long over, or one that never had to be had at all. But for so long as it is necessary, I will never for a moment discount the privilege of being a part of such an important moment in history.

Perseverance doesn't always look like a triumphant speech from a podium. It doesn't always look like a tearful awards ceremony or a Grammy Awards shout-out. Sometimes it looks like a morning when you don't get out of bed. Sometimes it looks like a bout of sobbing, not because you spilled your drink but because everything is just *so much* and that drink pushed you past your threshold. Sometimes it looks like a moment when you sit, take a deep breath, and think about how exhausted you are.

It can look like your best of days, or your worst of days.

What matters is that there are more days. Visibility has been important in this fight, but the quiet efforts of the trans youth all across the nation are also important. Trans youth who dare to be themselves. They interact in their communities and make a difference that way. They come out in their schools and make a difference that way. They speak to their congressmen and congresswomen about safety and accessibility and make a difference that way. Or they live quietly and try to stay under the radar for their own protection and safety. Even this makes a difference. It makes a difference because all of it is perseverance. Each time a transgender youth puts one foot in front of the other, it is perseverance.

Enormous progress has been made in the conversation surrounding not only bathroom access for trans youth, but also a greater acceptance and support of all trans people. Even negative rulings are a positive thing: they mean that the platform is there for transgender people to be heard. Only five or ten years ago, that platform did not exist at all. Perseverance got us to this point. It will be difficult, and it will be long, but perseverance will eventually get us to a world in which no one has to prepare themselves for their day because of an administration hostile to who they are.

 Gavin Grimm is a transgender activist and ACLU plaintiff fighting for equality for trans students.

BIOGRAPHIES OF CONTRIBUTORS

Auontai "Tay" Anderson, a former candidate for the Denver Public Schools Board of Education, was, at eighteen, the youngest person to run for public office in Colorado. His passion and perseverance come from his grandmother, who has spent the past six years in the hospital. Tay plans to make her proud by taking everything she has instilled in him and—with the education Denver's schools provided him—working for the benefit of all students in the fight for public education.

Azure Antoinette has been called "the Maya Angelou of the millennial generation." She is a poet, an entrepreneur, and a millennial and arts education advocate.

Binta Niambi Brown is the founder of Big Mouth Records, a start-up that is innovating a new business model for the music industry, and manages Grammy Award–winning singer Grace

Weber. She has been selected as a Young Global Leader by the World Economic Forum and named to the *Financial Times'* EMpower 100 Ethnic Minority Leaders, *Fortune's* 40 Under 40, the Root's 100 Most Influential African Americans, *Crain's New York Business's* 40 Under 40, and *Jet's* 40 Under 40.

Matthew Burgess is an assistant professor at Brooklyn College. He is the author of a poetry collection, *Slippers for Elsewhere* (UpSet Press, 2014), and a children's book, *Enormous Small-ness: A Story of E. E. Cummings* (Enchanted Lion Books, 2015), which was named one of the best children's books of the year by the *Washington Post,* the *Boston Globe,* and *HuffPost.* He has edited an anthology of visual art and writing titled *Dream Closet: Meditations on Childhood Space* (Secretary Press, 2016) and has two children's books forthcoming: *Drawing on Walls: A Story of Keith Haring* (Enchanted Lion Books, 2018) and *The Unbudgeable Curmudgeon* (Knopf, 2019).

Kenyon Catchings is a sales executive with over ten years of experience servicing multiple specialties, including ophthalmology, primary care, psychiatry, neurology, endocrinology, and pain management. He is the proud father of four sons: Maleek, Kale, Jayce, and Jamison.

Tamika Catchings is a four-time Olympic gold medalist and sixteen-year WNBA superstar with the Indiana Fever. The twelve-time all-WNBA selection and ten-time WNBA all-star helped lead the Fever to a league-record twelve consecutive playoff appearances and thirteen playoff appearances overall. She was the 2011 league MVP and the 2012 finals MVP and was named the WNBA Defensive Player of the Year an unprecedented five times. She is the leading rebounder in WNBA history and its number three all-time scorer. ESPN named Tamika the inaugural Sports Humanitarian of the Year in 2015; she is also a two-time recipient of the WNBA's Dawn Staley Community Leadership Award and the first three-time winner of the WNBA's Kim Perrot Sportsmanship Award. She currently serves as director of player programs and franchise development for Pacers Sports & Entertainment, a role that includes work with the Indiana Pacers, the Indiana Fever, and the Fort Wayne Mad Ants. She is the daughter of former NBA star Harvey Catchings; her sister Tauja was drafted by the Phoenix Mercury in 2000. Tamika and Tauja established the Catch the Stars Foundation in 2004.

Tauja Catchings is the executive director of the Catch the Stars Foundation and resides in Brownsburg, Indiana, with her husband, Tim, and their sons, Kanon and Kolton.

Maneet Chauhan is an internationally recognized cookbook author, a TV personality, an active philanthropist, and the chef and owner of Chauhan Ale & Masala House in Nashville, Tennessee. She is a James Beard Foundation Award recipient most recently known for her work on Food Network's *Chopped*, for which she sits on the permanent panel of judges. She also competed on *Iron Chef America*, against Masaharu Morimoto, and on *The Next Iron Chef.*

Soraya Chemaly is a writer and an activist whose work focuses on the role of gender in culture, politics, religion, and media. She is the director of the Women's Media Center Speech Project, which is involved in curbing online abuse, promoting media and tech diversity, and expanding women's freedom of expression. Her work has appeared in *Time,* the *Guardian,* the *Nation,* and the *Atlantic* and on *HuffPost* and Role Reboot. In 2013, Soraya won the Association for Education in Journalism and Mass Communication's Donna Allen Award for Feminist Advocacy. In 2015, she was named one of *Elle*'s 25 Inspiring Women to Follow on Twitter. Follow Soraya on Twitter at @schemaly.

 Amy Chu is currently writing the KISS and Red Sonja comic series, having wrapped up Poison Ivy's first-ever miniseries for DC Comics. She has also written stories featuring Ant-Man and Deadpool for Marvel. Other stories she's written and series she's contributed to include *The X-Files: Deviations* (IDW), *Sensation Comics Featuring Wonder Woman* (DC), *CBLDF Liberty Annual* (Image Comics), and *Vertigo Quarterly: CMYK* (DC). Amy also writes and produces comics for nonprofits including the New-York Historical Society, the Baltimore Museum of Art, Pop Culture Classroom, and the Museum of Chinese in America.

 Jarron Collins pursued his academic and athletic endeavors at Stanford University, where he received the Howie Dallmar Coaches Award and was a finalist for the John R. Wooden Award, which is presented annually to the most outstanding college basketball player in the United States, based on performance and character. The Utah Jazz selected Jarron with the fifty-third pick in the 2001 NBA draft; he became one of only ten players to spend eight or more seasons with the Jazz, reaching the Western Conference finals with them. He subsequently played with the Phoenix Suns, the Los Angeles Clippers, the Portland Trail Blazers, and the Qingdao Eagles in China. He is currently entering his third year as an assistant coach with the Golden State Warriors. Along with his twin brother, Jason, Jarron gave a speech at the Democratic National Convention in 2016.

 Jason Collins is a former NBA player. He attended Stanford University, where he was an All-American in the 2000–2001 season. Upon graduating, he was the eighteenth overall pick in the first round of the 2001 NBA draft. In his thirteen-year career, Jason played center for six teams: the Nets (in both New Jersey and Brooklyn), the Memphis Grizzlies, the Minnesota Timberwolves, the Atlanta Hawks, the Boston Celtics, and the Washington Wizards. After the 2012–2013 NBA season concluded, he came out as gay in a cover story for *Sports Illustrated,* becoming the first male active player in any of the four major American professional sports leagues to come out publicly. Jason has traveled the country with the mission of empowering people to live their lives as their true selves and has become an active member of numerous charities, foundations, and organizations. In April 2014, he was featured on the cover of *Time* as one of its 100 Most Influential People. He is also an ambassador for NBA Cares, spreading goodwill on behalf of the NBA with its players, community, and corporate partners.

J. W. Cortés is an award-winning actor, a marine combat veteran, a singer, and a philanthropist. Born in Brooklyn, New York, and raised there by inspirational Puerto Rican parents, he developed an interest in the arts along with a desire to serve his community and country. Currently playing the recurring role of Detective Carlos Alvarez on Fox's hit prime-time series *Gotham,* he is the first actor to portray the iconic comic-book character on-screen. When he isn't performing or serving as a real-life police officer, he is engaged as a board member for Got Your 6 and the Detective Rafael Ramos Foundation. He loves interacting with his friends on all social media platforms and can be found at @jwcortes. *Photo credit: Charles Diaz*

 Wade Davis is a former NFL player. He is a thought leader, a writer, a public speaker, and an educator on gender, race, and orientation equality. Numerous professional sports leagues, including the National Hockey League, the Canadian Football League, and Major League Soccer, rely on him to provide guidance on matters of inclusion at the intersection of sexism and homophobia. Wade is dedicated to using his platforms and social currency to highlight issues affecting those most marginalized, including an intentional and specific focus on issues that directly impact women and girls; he collaborates regularly with the Ms. Foundation for Women, Planned Parenthood, and UN Women. He has spoken at or provided workshops and trainings for over one hundred colleges, universities, and corporations, nationally and internationally, including Stanford University, Penn State, Syracuse University, Texas A&M University, Fox, PepsiCo, JPMorgan Chase, Goldman Sachs, and Deutsche Bank.

Amy Fox is an acclaimed screenwriter, playwright, and educator and a passionate advocate for elevating women's voices in the arts and the workplace. Most recently, she wrote the screenplay for *Equity*, a female-driven Wall Street film that premiered at Sundance in 2016 and was released by Sony Pictures Classics. Her work has been recognized by the Alfred P. Sloan Foundation, the Kilroys, and Women's Image Network and honored with the Susan Smith Blackburn Prize. Amy teaches screenwriting for New York University's graduate film program. She lives in Brooklyn, New York, with her husband and two children. She is originally from Boulder, Colorado. Learn more about Amy at amyfox.net or on Twitter at @amylaurenfox.

 Shruti Ganguly is an award-winning filmmaker based in New York City. She has worked with Rabbit Bandini Productions for the past seven years and has made several feature films that have gone to the Sundance, Venice, Berlin, Telluride, and AFI film festivals. She was a founding partner at Fictionless, a production company that focuses on documentaries, TV series, and branded content. She is currently producing a feature with Keanu Reeves and is developing several other scripted films and TV series, including *Girly* with Refinery29 and Rashida Jones. Shruti recently launched her own production and media company, Honto88, which focuses on scripted film and television, narrative features, and videos through the lens of social responsibility. She will be directing her first feature, *Eternal Buzz*, next year.

Jadaida Glover is a graduate of the High School for Medical Professions in Brooklyn, New York. She writes poetry that is from the point of view of someone else, which she would describe as storytelling with a poetic twist. She was a mentee at Girls Write Now for two years and is now a student at Nyack College in New York. To learn about Girls Write Now, visit GirlsWriteNow.com.

Photo credit: Katherine Jacobs

Jeff Gomez turned his love of Japanese anime and epic fantasy novels into one of the greatest jobs in the universe. He works as a producer in charge of taking huge science-fiction and fantasy franchises and extending their story worlds across movies, comic books, video games, novels, and apps. Jeff founded Starlight Runner Entertainment and has become one of the world's leading "transmedia storytellers." Realizing his dream of working in Hollywood, Jeff collaborated with Disney on *Pirates of the Caribbean,* with James Cameron on *Avatar,* with 343 Industries on *Halo,* and with Will Smith on *Men in Black.* He works with inner-city kids through his program Never Surrender! and shares his experiences with obsessive-compulsive disorder with young people who are on the OCD and autism spectrums. He is also adapting his transmedia skills to help communities and nations in crisis across the globe. His transmedia population activation techniques and new storytelling model, which he calls Collective Journey, have been used in Mexico, Colombia, Australia, North Africa, and the Middle East. Jeff now lives in Manhattan with his wife, Chrysoula, and their daughter, Evangelia. Follow him on Facebook at facebook.com/transmedia, on Twitter at @jeff_gomez, and on Instagram at @slrgomez.

Soulaima Gourani is a speaker, an author, and a special adviser to ministers, task forces, government think tanks, and private companies all over the world. She has dedicated her life to improving the lives of others.

Gavin Grimm is a transgender activist and ACLU plaintiff fighting for equality for trans students. He was named one of the 30 Most Influential Teens and the 100 Most Influential People by *Time* and an OUTstanding Virginian by Equality Virginia; he also won the Courage Award at the Village Voice Pride Awards, the Andrew Cray Award from the National Center for Transgender Equality, and the Gerald B. Roemer Community Service Award from the US Department of Justice. *Photo credit: ACLU and Scout Tufankjian*

Leslie Herod represents northeast Denver in the Colorado House of Representatives. She is the first African American LGBT candidate elected to the state legislature. She is a champion for civil and reproductive rights and is committed to building a more just, inclusive, and prosperous Colorado. She currently serves on the House Judiciary and Finance Committees and the Joint Committee on Legal Services.

Patrisse Khan-Cullors is an artist, an organizer, and a freedom fighter from Los Angeles, California. A cofounder of Black Lives Matter, she is also a performance artist, a Fulbright scholar, a public speaker, and an NAACP History Maker. She's received many awards for activism and movement building, including being named a civil rights leader for the twenty-first century by the *Los Angeles Times* and a 2016 Glamour Woman of the Year.

US Senator Amy Klobuchar is the first woman elected to represent Minnesota in the United States Senate.

Sally Kohn is one of the leading progressive voices in America today. Currently a CNN political commentator and columnist, she is the author of *The Opposite of Hate* (Algonquin, 2018)—about why there's so much hate in our world today, why it's getting worse, and what we can do to stop it.

James Lecesne is a cofounder of the Trevor Project, the only nationwide twenty-four-hour suicide prevention and crisis intervention lifeline for LGBTQ youth. He wrote the screenplay for the Academy Award–winning short film *Trevor*, which inspired the founding of the Trevor Project. He has created several solo shows, including *Word of Mouth, One Man Band,* and *The Absolute Brightness of Leonard Pelkey.* His ensemble play *The Road Home: Stories of the Children of War* was presented worldwide. He has written three novels, including *Absolute Brightness* (Macmillan, 2008), and he was the executive producer of *After the Storm,* a feature-length documentary film that follows the lives of twelve young people living in post-Katrina New Orleans. *Photo credit: Matthew Murphy*

Jess Markt is the disability sport and integration adviser for the International Committee of the Red Cross. He coaches the Denver Rolling Nuggets of the National Wheelchair Basketball Association when he's not traveling around the world with the Red Cross, starting sports programs for physically disabled people in war and conflict zones. *Photo credit: International Wheelchair Basketball Federation*

Melissa Marr is a *New York Times* bestselling author of award-winning novels, picture books, and short fiction. Prior to writing, she taught literature and gender studies. Currently, she lives and writes in the Arizona desert and teaches beginners historical German long sword in her free time. You can reach her on Twitter at @melissa_marr.

Xiuhtezcatl Martinez (pronounced *shoo-tez-caht*) is a teenage indigenous climate activist, a hip-hop artist, and a powerful voice on the front lines of a global youth-led environmental movement. He began speaking around the world at the age of six; since then, he has addressed audiences everywhere from the United Nations Conference on Sustainable Development, Rio+20, in Brazil to the UN headquarters in New York City. He has been featured on *Real Time with Bill Maher, Skavlan,* PBS, Showtime, National Geographic, Upworthy, Al Jazeera, AJ+, CNN, MSNBC, and HBO, and in *Vice, Rolling Stone,* the *Guardian, Vogue,* and more. In 2013, Xiuhtezcatl was the youngest of the Top 24 Under 24 Youth Changemakers chosen by the Campaign for a Presidential Youth Council. He was honored with a 2015 Peace First Prize, the 2016 Young Superhero for Earth Award from Captain

Planet Foundation, and the 2016 Children's Climate Prize from Sweden.

Erin McKeown is a musician, writer, and producer known internationally for her prolific disregard of stylistic boundaries. She is a familiar presence on NPR and the BBC, and her songs have also been featured in many television shows and commercials. An active voice on social justice issues and culture, Erin was a 2011–2012 fellow at the Berkman Klein Center for Internet & Society at Harvard University, and she has also worked closely with a range of nonprofits focusing on her core concerns of media justice and immigration reform. Her first original musical, written with Pulitzer Prize–winning playwright Quiara Alegría Hudes, premiered in 2016 at La Jolla Playhouse. Her latest album is 2017's *Mirrors Break Back*. Learn more at ErinMcKeown.com. *Photo credit: Jo Chattman*

Leland Melvin is a former astronaut and NFL player, an educator, a photographer, and a musician. Before becoming an astronaut, he played professional football with the Detroit Lions and the Dallas Cowboys. He received a BS in chemistry and an MS in materials science engineering, then traveled off-planet twice on the space shuttle *Atlantis* to help build the International Space Station. Upon hanging up his space boots, he led NASA Education and cochaired the White House's Federal Coordination in STEM Education Task Force, developing the nation's five-year plan for science, technology, engineering, and math education. After twenty-four years with NASA as a researcher, astronaut, and senior executive service leader, Leland now shares stories of his life as an athlete, an astronaut, a scientist, an engineer, a photographer, and a musician to help inspire the next generation of explorers to pursue careers in science, technology, engineering, art, and math. *Photo credit: NASA*

 Jillian Mercado is the most recognizable model with muscular dystrophy and has worked with multiple industry icons. She has appeared on various television shows, including *E! News,* and been praised for both her modeling and her representation of the differently abled in fashion. To date, Jillian has starred in campaigns for Nordstrom and Target, as well as editorial features in *Glamour* and *Cosmopolitan* magazines. She was also shot by Michael Avedon for Carine Roitfeld's *CR Fashion Book.* In 2016, she appeared in the merchandising campaign for Beyoncé's Formation world tour, launching a new episode in her modeling career. Most recently, she graced the cover of *Glassbook* magazine. "I'm showing that having a disability doesn't have to be ugly, and how it should be embraced. I wish I had that role model growing up, but to be that role model is great." *Photo credit: Peeta Martinez*

 Prisca Dorcas Mojica Rodriguez was born in Managua, Nicaragua, but now calls Nashville, Tennessee, home. She is currently working on a children's book, because as a brown girl who never saw herself represented, she seeks to provide more representation for young black and brown girls. She started the online platform Latina Rebels in 2013, which now boasts over two hundred thousand followers. She has been featured on Telemundo, Univision, Mitú, *HuffPost Latino Voices,* Guerrilla Feminism, and

Everyday Feminism and in *Latina* and *Cosmopolitan,* and she was invited to the White House in the fall of 2016. She is unapologetic, angry, and uncompromising about protecting and upholding the stories of brown folks. *¡Que viva la gente!*

 Kiara Nirghin lives in Johannesburg, South Africa. In 2016, at sixteen, she won the Google Science Fair, and its Community Impact Award for the Middle East and Africa, with her invention No More Thirsty Crops. The idea stemmed from the fact that South Africa and other nearby countries are suffering from the worst drought the region has seen in over twenty years. The award included a scholarship and placed her on *Time*'s list of the 30 Most Influential Teens. She is a student ambassador for the World Wildlife Fund, was nominated as a Global Teen Leader as part of the Three Dot Dash initiative, and has been invited to speak at TEDx and *Forbes Woman Africa* events. Kiara is currently continuing her research as a scientist and hopes to encourage other young scientists to make an impact on the world around them.

 Maulik Pancholy is best known for playing Jonathan on the classic Emmy-, Golden Globe–, and Screen Actors Guild Award–winning NBC comedy *30 Rock.* He is also widely recognized for playing Sanjay on the Showtime hit series *Weeds* and Neal on the first season of the NBC comedy *Whitney.* He was the voice of Baljeet on over one hundred episodes of Disney's *Phineas and Ferb* and the voice of Sanjay on the Nickelodeon animated series *Sanjay and Craig*—the first lead Indian American character on a network cartoon. In 2014, President Barack Obama appointed Maulik to serve on the President's Advisory Commission on Asian Americans and Pacific Islanders. During his nearly three-year tenure as a commissioner, Maulik helped launch an anti-bullying campaign called #ActToChange, designed to meet the needs of young Asian Americans and Pacific Islanders.

 Alysia Reiner is an actress, a producer, an activist, and a consummate Pollyanna who uses her superpowers for good. She won a Screen Actors Guild ensemble award for her portrayal of Natalie "Fig" Figueroa on *Orange Is the New Black*. She also plays Sunny on FX's Peabody Award–winning *Better Things* and has appeared on *How to Get Away with Murder, Odd Mom Out, Search Party, Younger,* and *Broad City*. Alysia starred in the film *Equity,* which she also produced. She loves working as a change maker for women and has been invited to the White House, the United Nations, SHE Summit, Google, and Cannes Lions to speak about breaking barriers for women. She's been honored with a Persistence of Vision Award by the Women's Media Summit, a Sarah Powell Huntington Leadership Award by the Women's Prison Association, a Voice of a Woman Award, a Pioneer in Filmmaking Award by the New Hampshire Film Festival, and a Founders Award for Support by the Cancer Support Community. She is a graduate of Vassar College. Follow Alysia on Twitter at @alysiareiner.

 Vicki Saunders is an entrepreneur, an award-winning mentor, an adviser to the next generation of change makers, and a leading advocate for entrepreneurship as a way of creating positive transformation in the world. She is the founder of SheEO and

#RadicalGenerosity, a global initiative to radically transform how female entrepreneurs are supported, financed, and celebrated. She has cofounded and run ventures in Europe, Canada, and the United States and taken a company public on the Toronto Stock Exchange. Vicki was called one of the 100 most influential leaders of 2015 by the movement Empowering a Billion Women by 2020. In 2001, she was named a Global Leader for Tomorrow by the World Economic Forum.

Dr. Gail Schoettler has been a US ambassador, Colorado's lieutenant governor and state treasurer, Douglas County's school board president, and a businesswoman. She narrowly lost her race for governor of Colorado, and she was a founder of the Women's Bank of Denver. She graduated from Stanford University with a BS in economics and earned both an MA and a PhD in African history from the University of California, Santa Barbara. Among her many awards is the Legion of Honor, France's highest civilian award. She cofounded Electing Women and the Electing Women Alliance to get women involved in raising money for women running for governor and US senator across the country, strongly believing that when women support women, women win. She is an avid hiker who has conquered her fear of heights to climb all fifty-four of Colorado's fourteen-thousand-foot peaks and nineteen-thousand-foot Mount Kilimanjaro.

Alia Shawkat currently stars in the TBS series *Search Party*. She can also be seen in the thriller *Green Room* and the Netflix film *Pee-wee's Big Holiday*. Her other feature credits include *Paint It*

Black, Nasty Baby, Wild Canaries, Night Moves, The To Do List, The Final Girls, Me Him Her, The Driftless Area, 20th Century Women, and *Izzy Gets the F*ck Across Town.* She is well known for her role as Maeby Fünke in the cult series *Arrested Development* and has also appeared on Comedy Central's *Broad City* and HBO's *Getting On.* Alia is also a talented jazz singer and pianist and an accomplished painter and illustrator.

Imran Siddiquee is a writer, a filmmaker, and an activist working to transform how gender and race are represented in the media. He helped start the Representation Project, where he worked on documentary films and led large-scale campaigns to call out sexism in the media. In 2014, he gave a TEDx talk called "How Hollywood Can Tell Better Love Stories," and his 2015 short film *Love Reset* was produced by MTV. His writing has been published by the *Atlantic, BuzzFeed, Salon,* and other online publications.

Jesselyn Silva is a twelve-year-old boxer who lives with her brother and dad in Bergenfield, New Jersey. When she's not in the boxing gym, she's reading, drawing, playing sports, or building with Lego bricks.

Johnny Silvercloud is an abolitionist photographer, writer, and speaker who cares deeply about the self-care of people of color, especially black folks. You can learn more about him at AfroSapiophile.com.

Nate Smith has helped reinvigorate the international jazz scene with his visceral style of drumming, playing with such leading lights as bassist Dave Holland, saxophonists Chris Potter and Ravi Coltrane, and singers Patricia Barber, Somi, and José James. On his bandleader debut, *Kinfolk: Postcards from Everywhere* (Waterbaby Music/Ropeadope, 2017), he fuses his original modern jazz compositions with R&B, pop, and hip-hop. The *New York Times* described Nate as "a firecracker of a drummer." The *Village Voice* described him as "superlative . . . a one-man band on drums and programming." He is also an esteemed and experienced educator, teaching master classes and drum clinics all over the globe.

 Fanny Starr is a Holocaust survivor. She was born in Lodz, Poland, in 1922. In 1939, the Nazis moved her family into the Lodz Ghetto, where she lived for five years, until being transported to Auschwitz in 1944. Later, she was sent to Ravensbrück; to a factory in Mühlhausen, Germany; and finally to Bergen-Belsen, where she met her husband. She was liberated from Bergen-Belsen on April 15, 1945. Fanny has lived in Denver for sixty years and is the mother of three children.

 José Antonio Tijerino is the president of the Hispanic Heritage Foundation.

Danielle Vabner lost her six-year-old brother, Noah, in the Sandy Hook school shooting on December 14, 2012. He was killed along with nineteen of his classmates and six educators. In the years since, she has become a passionate advocate for gun violence prevention, and she hopes to honor her brother's life by fighting the good fight.

 Pej Vahdat is an actor who was born in Tehran, Iran, and raised in San Jose, California. He grew up playing tennis, and continued to play at San Diego State University, from which he graduated with a degree in business with a minor in theater arts. He has appeared on many television shows, including *Shameless, Bones,* and *Sneaky Pete,* and, most recently, in the Denzel Washington film *Roman J. Israel, Esq.* He resides in Los Angeles with his girlfriend and two dogs.

 Patricia Valoy is the science and social justice managing editor of the Praxis Center and a feminist activist, consultant, writer, and speaker on diversity and gender in science, technology, engineering, and math (STEM). She holds a BS in civil engineering from Columbia University, where she focused on construction management and structural engineering. She writes and speaks about a variety of issues pertaining to women in STEM and other male-dominated fields, particularly as they relate to women of color and underrepresented minorities. Patricia's advocacy is focused on attracting women to STEM careers, retaining them, and building work environments where they are free from discrimination, sexism, and racism. She also speaks and writes on issues affecting the Latino community, including racism, immigration, cultural and religious pressures, and living at the intersection of two cultures.

 Liz Wolfson, the fourth child in a family of competitive athletes, was reared on a backyard basketball court, where she learned how to use both hands for layups and to never let her brothers knock her down. Always the quiet rebel, Liz hated being told what to do by anybody and decided not to settle on the career path in organizational management that was set before her. At age forty, with a newborn in her arms, she thought it the perfect time to start up her dream project, which would model for her children what it means to envision, create, struggle, and succeed. Feeling that the educational opportunities for girls in America were insufficient to match the reality of growing up in today's world, Liz became the chief visionary officer of Girls Athletic Leadership Schools, a game-changing educational model focused on positive gender identity and integrated movement.

DISCUSSION QUESTIONS

1. The title of this anthology, *Nevertheless, We Persisted,* is also its main theme. The phrase *nevertheless, she persisted* was used in reference to Senator Elizabeth Warren, who in 2017 refused to stop testifying on the Senate floor, even in the face of admonition from her (mostly) male colleagues. Why do you think these words have such resonance across our culture today? In what ways do the authors of these essays demonstrate persistence? What strengths and supports does a person require in order to be persistent?

2. Readers of these essays gain insight into the experiences and inner feelings of the authors and the reasons for their actions. In coming to understand another person in such a specific and detailed way, it is easy to develop empathy for that person. Talk about an example in an essay in which a person in power did not have empathy for the author. What barriers in daily life prevent us from developing empathy for other people? What circumstances need to be in place in order for empathy between people to emerge? Why does empathy matter?

3. Close your eyes and imagine a room full of people who are different from you. Who is there, and in what ways are those people different from you? Are they different in terms of race? Religion? Gender? Physical ability? Consider what this reveals about your subconscious ideas of "difference." What kinds of people are *not* in the room, and what does their absence mean? In what ways might those subconscious ideas manifest in daily life? How might acknowledging that we all have subconscious ideas about difference change our behavior?

4. Think of an author of one of the essays whose life circumstances have been very different from your own. Have you ever encountered a person with that identity in your own life? If you haven't, what do you think prevented that from happening? Which factors that keep you from meeting and getting to know people different from you are in your control? Which are not? What value is there in coming to understand the experiences of people who are different from you?

5. Elie Wiesel said, "The opposite of love is not hate, it's indifference." In many of these essays, people witnessed actions that were clearly harmful to the authors but didn't act to protect them. What do you imagine kept them from acting? What makes it difficult to step in when you witness discrimination in action?

6. What themes in the essays did you notice that were shared across different experiences and identities? What do those shared themes tell us about the way having certain identities influences our lives? What do those themes tell us about the culture we are living in?

7. Many of the people surrounding the authors displayed good intentions, and yet some of them caused great harm. Talk about an example in which a person's intentions were different from the impact of their words or actions. What were the ways their good intentions impeded them from seeing where they inflicted hurt? Think of an example from the essays in which a person with good intentions acted in a way that was informed by unconscious bias. What would have needed to change in order for that person's impact to have matched their intentions?

8. Choose an essay that stood out to you and discuss what about it touched your curiosity or emotions. Why do you think that essay belongs in this anthology? What challenges did the author have to overcome in order to persist? How did he or she go about persisting? What does the essay mean to you? If you could send a message to the author, what would you want to say?

9. Many of the essays in this anthology were written by adults reflecting on their childhood or adolescence. Why do you think issues of identity come up so strongly in childhood and adolescence? Talk about an example that stood out to you in which aspects of an author's identity shifted over time. In what ways did that shift come from within, with the author changing how he or she saw himself or herself? In what ways did the change come from an external source, in response to how the author was seen by others? How has your identity changed over time?

10. *Intersectionality* is a term that describes how various aspects of a person's identity intersect to construct experience. For example,

being black and a woman is related to, but different from, being white and a woman. Talk about an essay that illustrates how the intersection of different identities influences a person's experience. How do aspects of identity like race, class, gender, and sexuality intersect? Why is intersectionality a helpful concept in thinking about social justice?

11. Think about an aspect of your own identity that affords you a certain kind of advantage in life. What advantages does that identity give you? What kind of identity is more privileged than yours? In what ways? What identities afford fewer privileges? In what ways? Discuss ways in which you see privilege emerging as a theme in the anthology. Why is privilege important to talk about in the context of social justice?

12. In "As Is," Alysia Reiner shares her internal expressions of self-doubt and insecurity, even from her current place of fame. How did you feel as you read that voice? In what ways did that self-critical voice feel familiar to you? How are messages of "not good enough," in all their forms, conveyed? What does it take to overcome that inner voice of uncertainty?

13. In "Nevertheless, Love Persists," Danielle Vabner gives an account of the day her brother was killed in the Sandy Hook Elementary School shooting. Discuss how you imagine speaking out on her brother's behalf affects her. In what ways might it help her cope? In what ways might it be painful? What are ways for activists and advocates to care for themselves and each other as they go about their work? Why is paying particular attention to self-care important as people persist through hardship?

14. In "The Practice of Self-Love," Wade Davis shares his memory of how he treated an openly gay classmate, John Smith, in high school. How do you imagine John's memories of high school feel? If John had realized the influence he had on Wade's life, do you think that would have helped or further hurt him? How did playing the role of bully influence Wade's feelings about himself? How does insight from the bully's perspective change how you think about the problem of bullying?

15. In "#NoFilter," Azure Antoinette talks about the reflexive ease with which her mother taught her to code-switch. What did she later discover she gave up in learning to do so? Are there instances in your life when you have to put on an affectation in order to fit in? What gifts does code-switching offer? What consequences does it incur? What does it mean to be a person who hasn't had the need to code-switch?

16. In "Reflections of a Younger Silvercloud," Johnny Silvercloud weaves together the historical underpinnings of racism in the United States with his lived experiences of it. Was there a moment in the essay when you as a reader found yourself considering explanations other than racism as the cause of his experiences? Why did you respond that way? How do you think your own racial identity influences how you read this essay?

17. In "Sometimes You Are Better Off Not Knowing," Binta Niambi Brown recalls being fueled by a sense of obligation to others like her as she fought against a racist supervisor in her firm. Do you think it was her responsibility to think about those others as she considered her actions? In what ways is having such

a responsibility a gift? In what ways might it be a burden? Have you had the responsibility of being an example to others who share your identity? If so, what was that like? If not, why do you think this is not a part of your experience?

Discussion questions prepared by Jennifer Sarche.

COPYRIGHT INFORMATION

INDEX

305